A Tutor's Guide

HELPING WRITERS
ONE TO ONE

2ND
EDITION

edited by BEN RAFOTH

Boynton/Cook Publishers
HEINEMANN
Portsmouth, NH

Boynton/Cook Publishers, Inc.

361 Hanover Street
Portsmouth, NH 03801–3912
www.boyntoncook.com

© 2005, 2000 by Boynton/Cook Publishers

Library of Congress Cataloging-in-Publication Data
A tutor's guide : helping writers one to one / edited by Ben Rafoth. —2nd ed.
   p. cm.
  Includes bibliographical references and index.
  ISBN 0-86709-587-3 (acid-free paper)
   1. English language—Rhetoric—Study and teaching. 2. Report writing—Study and teaching (Higher). 3. Tutors and tutoring. I. Rafoth, Bennett A. II. Title.

  PE1404.T885 2005
  808′.042′071—dc22   2005012543

Editor: Lisa Luedeke
Production: Vicki Kasabian
Cover design: Catherine Hawkes, Cat & Mouse
Typesetter: TechBooks
Manufacturing: Louise Richardson

Printed in the United States of America on acid-free paper
15 14 13 12 11 VP 7 8 9 10 11

Contents

Tutors need to learn from international students in order to help them, and international students need to learn from tutors in order to become better writers in English. Making contact is where it all begins.

Acknowledgments

I would like to thank many people for their support and encouragement along the way, but most especially the contributors to this book, who made it all possible. Thanks also to the National Conference on Peer Tutoring in Writing, especially the 1998 conferees at SUNY Plattsburgh, some of whom are represented in this collection, to Katie Bailey and Doug Tucker for help with typing and proofreading, to Jen Ritter for website design and typing, to Lisa Luedeke, my editor at Heinemann Boynton/Cook, whose encouragement and guidance have been invaluable, and to my family for love and kindness always, Mary Ann, Henry, and Paige.

Introduction

This second edition of *A Tutor's Guide* builds on the strengths that made the first edition so well received among tutors. One-third of the book is new material. Five new chapters add themes readers will appreciate:

- Exploring cultural issues involved in working with ESL writers
- Helping students in professional writing courses
- Meeting the needs of students in advanced writing classes
- Working in a graduate writing center
- Imagining how to save a tutoring session gone awry

The focus of the book remains the same—to take everyday events in tutoring sessions and connect them to theory and good practice. In these pages, tutors will find conflicting ideas and glimpses of theoretical debates that enliven tutoring and make it endlessly interesting. Like the first edition, the second edition helps tutors to think through and deal with common problems that arise in tutoring sessions. It encourages the exercise of good judgment and effective practices.

This edition of *A Tutor's Guide* opens the door to some of the professional conversation that surrounds writing center practices. At the same time, it offers concrete suggestions, things to try, and problems to think about for the next tutoring session. Each of the chapters in this collection, except for Chapter 3, which reads more as a case study for discussion, follows a similar organization:

- *Introduction*—Describes a problem or concern tutors are likely to encounter in writing conferences, like trying to engage a reluctant writer or helping to make a paper more creative.
- *Some Background*—Provides a context for the problem based in the professional literature.
- *What to Do*—Offers concrete suggestions for how to approach the session, and what to try when that doesn't work.
- *Complicating Matters*—Raises counterarguments and explores some of the complexities of learning to write, including reasons why best practices don't always pan out.

- *Further Reading*—Recommends helpful and interesting follow-up readings and provides a short description of each selection and its relevance for tutoring.
- *Notes and Works Cited*—A complete list of notes and references at the end of each chapter.

The authors who have contributed chapters to this edition of *A Tutor's Guide* have written for readers who are undergraduate or graduate students working part-time in a writing or tutorial center, students enrolled in undergraduate or graduate courses focused on teaching and tutoring writing, or writing teachers who are looking for ideas to improve writing conferences or peer review sessions. Most of all, the authors tried to imagine readers who can envision the tremendous potential of peer tutoring to help students become more engaged and thoughtful writers.

We all know that every tutoring session is unique, and that what works for one tutor or writer may not help at all in a different set of circumstances. Even the way in which tutors and writers define *help* will vary. And yet, it is remarkable how much similarity does exist from one session to another, and how much agreement there is about what constitutes effective and ineffective tutoring practices. These chapters in *A Tutor's Guide* build on this agreement. They create a motivating dissatisfaction, a desire to help tutors meet the challenges that arise when they sit down to help writers.

A final note   Wendy Bishop, who contributed the chapter "Is There a Creative Writer in the House?" died on November 21, 2003. During her distinguished career, Wendy wrote more than twenty-two books and numerous articles, poems, and short stories. She was Kellogg W. Hunt Distinguished Professor of English at Florida State University and, before that, worked in the writing center at the University of Alaska. She was a keynote speaker at writing center conferences and was a friend to hundreds of tutors, students, writers, and teachers. Wendy's chapter appears unchanged from the first edition.

1

Setting the Agenda for the Next Thirty Minutes

William J. Macauley Jr.

When you meet a writer and sit down to talk about a paper, it might seem a little odd to make a plan for how you will spend the next thirty minutes together. But there's a worse problem: looking back at the past half hour and realizing you went practically nowhere with your tutoring session because you never really thought about where you wanted to end up. Every tutoring session needs a plan on which the writer and tutor can focus, even if you wind up changing it along the way or scrapping it completely.

I like to think of this plan like planning a trip with a road map. A road map is open ended in that it shows you many possible routes to travel, but the specific course you choose on the map never lets you forget that you're on a purposeful journey to your destination. Charting the course for a tutorial session is also a way to mark, simply and graphically, the things you want to do in the tutoring session: "Begin the session with _____, then _____, and conclude by _____." Fill in the blanks as you wish.

Years ago, I delivered a truckload of greeting card racks to a department store in Johnstown, Pennsylvania. I had been making my living as a local driver and it felt exciting to be going over-the-road. Shortly after crossing into Michigan, I pulled into Ma's Coffee Pot in the late afternoon before my trip and pored over the shiny new atlas I purchased there, computing the mileage and deciphering the lines, circles, dots, and colors that marked my route from Michigan to Pennsylvania. I then marked my route, got a good night's rest, and started out early the next morning.

Well, anyone who has ever driven on an expressway knows that having a map is no guarantee against wrong turns and traffic jams. Low bridges and narrow roadways are specifically a Pennsylvania problem; I learned that firsthand when I ended up backing the truck around blind corners and up hills, blowing my horn into the darkness, and turning around to find another road to Johnstown. But the route I marked with a yellow highlighter always kept me focused on where I had been and where I was headed.

More than once I tossed that atlas on the floor in frustration (truckers hate to ask for directions), but I finally backed up to the store's loading dock just before ten o'clock the next morning, road weary and sore. Two languishing humpers (freight handlers) met me in the parking lot, unloaded the racks from the truck, and I was off to the nearest Motel 6.

The point of this story is that planning a trip may not be the last place where a journey is negotiated; it does, however, give travelers a sense of perspective on where they are and where they want to end up. It is easy to lose this perspective during a tutoring session because the ideas in a conversation go by so quickly. My marked-up atlas kept me oriented and moving in the right direction even though it could not predict all the specific problems I encountered as I traveled; the map was necessary but not sufficient. It kept me aware of my options yet focused on my goal.

For a tutorial, charting a course for the session means setting the agenda for how you want the session to unfold. You and the writer might begin with a plan as simple as this:

Brainstorm (10 min) → Pick out main idea → Write thesis statement

Or your plan might be more elaborate, depicting problems the writer asked for help with early on, and others you decided to add after reading the rough draft. You could just make a list of these things, but mapping them out on a separate sheet with arrows (as I did) keeps the plan flexible (you can add to it easily) and gives it an appealing visual dimension. It is also a diagram that you and the student can make together.

Some Background

What I'm mainly talking about in this chapter is making a plan for the tutoring session, but you can also make one for the paper itself (like an outline). Many writing textbooks include substantial sections on planning an essay through tools such as:

- "building blocks"[1]
- clustering[2]
- mapping[3]
- outlining[4] or
- the "reporter's formula"[5]

Mapping, whether you do it for the whole paper or for the tutoring session, is a particular form of planning that lays out your main points and connects them with lines or arrows. It doesn't have to be hierarchical like an outline; instead, it can take the shape of a hub with spokes, a continuous circle, a tree, a flow-chart, or anything you want. It not only fixes a sequence of ideas or events in your mind but also provides a visual representation that can be used to help you stay on track—or take a jaunt. A tutorial map lets you point to the specific events you want to happen during the next thirty minutes, and you can add or delete a path, as well as insert placeholders, question marks, or reminders. You and your writer (Joe, in the following example) might make a plan for the session that looks something like this:

Think of illustration?

Decide how Joe's main idea compares with article's → Figure out *main diff* → Rewrite intro

Check quote

Like flowcharts and bar graphs, maps are visual representations using terms that do not have to be a part of the student's paper. So it's OK to jot down something like "Emphasize main diff" on a map until the writer figures out the exact words he wants to use in the paper. One of the advantages of drawing this kind of map in a tutorial is that it can be negotiated. When the map is negotiated, it is multivalent, meaning that both the tutor and writer can plan the tutorial cooperatively without either dominating the session or being tied unproductively to the writer's text. You can even think of the map as a third participant in the way it mediates the practice of the tutorial, affording an egalitarian or common space for working together and reminding us, as Paulo Freire says, that "Communion in turn elicits cooperation."[6]

Another way that tutorial maps function is to change the language options in the session. Tutors sometimes find themselves sounding like talking heads about writing because they don't really have a plan for approaching the writer's work and end up doling out generic advice ("Remember your audience," "Transitions are really key"). Student writers, by comparison, sometimes find it hard to apply what tutors say because the comments are not concrete enough. The opposite can happen, too: tutors can become editors because they don't know where else to begin, while students lose sight of their ideas because they get caught up in minutiae. When the agenda is set collaboratively with a map, however, the phases of the tutoring session are made explicit so that there's a better chance for mutual input and understanding. I hate to compare tutoring to going to a dentist, but I will anyway to make the point that I always want to know what my dentist plans to do before he does it, and I appreciate it when he loses the fancy medical jargon and just draws me a picture or shows me a diagram. I think the same holds true in the writing center: students want to know what's happening and they want to be part of decisions.

One more point. Tutors are often more skilled at conversing about writing than the clients they serve. For one thing, in the writing center we're on our home turf and they're not. As a visual representation, a map does not require conversational skill. If the writer has trouble speaking up or changing the topic, she can point to the map to signal her intent. Or, she can revise the map while you're talking or reading her paper. The map is always there to go back to.

Experienced tutors are adept at dealing with papers from many disciplines, courses, and teachers. But when tutors and writers map out a session, the plan can soon outlive its utility. So, while setting an agenda is useful for conceptualizing a journey based on available information, you can never know what the trip will be like until the rubber meets the road. How do you decide when to stick to the map and when to take a chance on an alternate route?

What to Do

Setting the agenda for the next thirty minutes (or forty-five–fifty if your writing center has longer sessions) will most likely be a variation on this general framework: Review the assignment, decide on the goals for the session, and finally, choose the best route to reach these goals.

Beginning

Before trying to build an agenda, ask open-ended questions about the paper and assignment. If you intend to encourage a student writer to take responsibility for writing, do so from the start of the session by asking him to tell you what he is thinking, what he wants. Is this the writer's first visit to the center? If so, begin by telling him about your writing center and how tutoring works. Then try to decide on the primary goal for the tutoring session. Is it to clarify some aspect of the assignment? To identify problems with the writer's supporting statements? To develop a stronger sounding voice? Exactly what is it that you hope to accomplish in thirty minutes? Write it on the top of a blank sheet of paper.

Setting the Agenda

Explore options for how to proceed. This is where your expertise as a writing tutor is really important. I recommend that you begin by inviting the writer to tell you how he would like to proceed. If this doesn't take you very far, suggest some options. Keep the primary goal in mind and look for the most direct route to reach it. (Other chapters in this book offer lots of ways to address specific problems and concerns that writers bring to the center.)

Draw the map together. Offer the writer a pen or marker, something with a cool color and an irresistible rollerball feel, but don't insist on it if the writer doesn't want to try it. Drawing a tutorial map is not everyone's idea of fun. Encourage the writer to help you name the points and connect them, yet realize that you may have to compress what she says into a map format.

Warn the writer of time constraints. This one is a little sneaky. Later in this stage, make sure that you tell the student that the two of you might not get to all of the points identified. Let the writer know that he may have to carry on alone, after the tutorial session has ended. This is when you tell him how use-ful the map will be later on. The sneaky part is that the agenda is almost more important for the writer's work after the tutorial has ended because the ulti-mate goal is always to enable the writer to work successfully without your help. You will have modeled how to make a plan, and this will go a long way in empowering the writer.

Complicating Matters[7]

In my truck, I was not constrained by how much vacation time I could afford. Rather, my travel was shaped by how long my employer expected the trip would take. This metaphor plays out in important ways for writers and tutors, too. A student is seldom working on only one project at a time, and the writer must have the opportunity to discuss time constraints. If the paper is due in twenty minutes, he doesn't really have time to explore the region; he just needs to know which exit to take.

I would encourage flexibility here and also warn that the faster the student drives, the more likely a crash. The urgency of the writing is often a result of not getting started early enough, and the tutorial session can often be a stu-dent's attempt to let a tutor make up for lost time. That lack of foresight is not the tutor's fault or problem; meanwhile, you still want to help. So, as a tutor, you have to decide where the cutoff is for you, at what point covering some ground is less important than facing the consequences of delay.

The student may view the tutorial as nothing more than a quick fix on the way to turning in the paper within the next hour. Is it more useful just to get him on his way or do you really want to tell him about the importance of pre-trip tire pressure inspections? If you try to push students beyond their time constraints, you run the risk of assuming too much responsibility for the stu-dents' work and turning the writers off to tutoring. This is an example of what Wingate (Chapter 2) calls "crossing the line." We would like everyone to be working through drafts with enough time to be thorough and thoughtful. Meanwhile, we know that this is often not the case. At times, we can almost see writers flashing their brights behind us, trying to get us to move out of their way. If we help them to move along, we may be able to get them into the serv-ice plaza again before their next trip.

Some student writers are just not interested in exploring their topics, regardless of the amount of time they have. They are focused on getting the paper done with sufficient success, like earning a B–. Gregory Clark suggests that this is the difference between a tourist and a traveler.

> Tourists engage only the places and people they can recognize as belonging
> within the boundaries of the territory they themselves occupy, but travelers
> leave that territory behind as they transform themselves in response to the
> necessities of the experience they encounter on the road.[8]

A writer may desire nothing more than returning to what is safe and familiar, like writing about how playing football builds character or how school uniforms deny individuality, and it may not always be productive to push a writer beyond his own planned route. You have to ask yourself, "Will pushing make him challenge himself and increase the likelihood of good writing?" In other words, what is the upshot of forcing a student into an adventure through the mountains when what he wants is a straight shot to the coast?

In *Zen and the Art of Motorcycle Maintenance,* Robert Pirsig talks about the Zen of motorcycling—knowing your vehicle, hearing and feeling the operating condition of the engine, and knowing the viscosity of the oil as the engine runs. Most writing tutors and teachers yearn for students to pay this kind of attention to writing, even though it would probably put them out of work. While it would be nice if everyone thought about writing with this sort of intensity, as a tutor you may feel that only you, not the writer, thinks about writing this way. In fact, you may be so attuned to what the writer needs to do that you skip the important step of spelling out the agenda and negotiating it with the writer. In other words, you may think, "If I know the problem is in the crankcase, why discuss it?"

But it's a mistake, really, to presume that you understand better than the writer what the session needs to be about. The map is not the tutorial. It is, rather, a plan for what the tutorial might be, a way of paying attention to one thing so that you can focus on another. And so what seems obvious to you may not be the case at all once you begin to see things from the writer's perspective. This is why negotiating the agenda and making the plan explicit is so important: It gives both of you a turn at the wheel.

Moreover, getting through the agenda may be less important than setting it because it is here that tough choices must be made. In thirty minutes, there may be only enough time to get to the first couple of points, but the writer leaves with a clear sense of what to do next. Ellen Barton observes, "reading and writing often play less of a role than the talk that comprises the encounter."[9] Planning the session thus becomes the means to helping the student work with her writing both now and later on, so that what happens in the writing center actually reaches into the student's future.

In order to meet the needs of both tutor and writer, that communion which Freire points to must be remembered. I would encourage three active and communal approaches. First, keep revising the map so that new considerations can emerge and be accommodated. Though mapping a tutorial is a very smart way to begin, the work of a tutorial is often not predictable enough to allow that map to remain essential throughout the session. Second, if the map becomes cumbersome, drop it. As I said before, the map is only as good as it is useful. Sometimes, it is better to explore than to plan. Finally, there may be times when the map is more useful than the writing the student has done. Let the writer take that map, make it her own, and hit the road.

Further Reading

Bruce, Shanti. 2004. "Getting Started." In *ESL Writers: A Guide for Writing Center Tutors*, eds. Shanti Bruce and Ben Rafoth, 30–38. Portsmouth, NH: Boynton/Cook.

Planning and prioritizing is especially important when working with ESL writers. Bruce offers helpful examples and advice for negotiating the agenda.

Flynn, Thomas, and Mary King. 1993. *Dynamics of the Writing Conference: Social and Cognitive Interaction*. Urbana, IL: NCTE.

This collection of essays accomplishes several goals important to agenda setting in tutorial sessions. First, it focuses on describing and promoting high-order concerns. Then it looks at collaborative writing from different perspectives. Tutors will appreciate the discussion of writing and writers in practical terms.

Murray, Donald M. 1995. *The Craft of Revision,* 2d ed. New York: Harcourt Brace.

This is a good book to read when you need ideas for planning the agenda with writers who seek help on problems in focusing, organizing, developing, reshaping, finding a voice, and editing. In a clear and entertaining style, this well-known author and writing teacher gives useful advice and concrete examples that will help you make suggestions and explore options to plan constructive tutoring sessions.

Rico, Gabriele Lusser. 1983. "Less Is More." In *Writing the Natural Way: Using Right-Brain Techniques to Release Your Expressive Powers*, 236–59. Boston: Houghton Mifflin.

This chapter is useful for tutors who want to use visual representations, like clustering, and it offers new ways of talking about topic, purpose, and audience, which writers will appreciate. This chapter is also quite helpful in the way it weaves together writing-to-learn, the entire process of writing, and the idea that there are multiple participants in each text.

Notes

1. Christine A. Hult and Thomas N. Huckin, *The New Century Handbook* (Boston: Allyn & Bacon, 1999).

2. Ann Raimes, *Keys for Writers: A Brief Handbook* (New York: Houghton Mifflin, 1999).

3. Leonard J. Rosen and Laurence Behrens, *The Allyn and Bacon Handbook*, 3d ed. (Boston: Allyn & Bacon, 1997).

4. Gary Columbo, Bonnie Lisle, and Sandra Mano, *Frame Work: Culture, Storytelling, and College Writing* (Boston: Bedford Books, 1997), 29.

5. Max Morenberg et al., *The Writer's Options: Lessons in Style and Arrangement*, 6th ed. (New York: Longman, 1999).

6. Paulo Freire, *Pedagogy of the Oppressed*. 20th anniversary ed. (New York: Continuum, 1994), 152.

7. I would like to acknowledge Janice Sebestyen's comments on an earlier draft as the basis for this section of the chapter.

8. Gregory Clark, "Writing as Travel, or Rhetoric on the Road." *College Composition and Communication* 49 (1) (1998): 16.

9. Ellen Barton, "Literacy in (Inter)Action." *College English* 59 (4) (1997): 409.

Works Cited

Barton, E. 1997. "Literacy in (Inter)Action." *College English* 59 (4): 408–37.

Clark, G. 1998. "Writing as Travel, or Rhetoric on the Road." *College Composition and Communication* 49 (1): 9–23.

Colombo, G., B. Lisle, and S. Mano. 1997. *Frame Work: Culture, Storytelling, and College Writing*. Boston: Bedford.

Freire, P. 1994. *Pedagogy of the Oppressed*. 20th anniversary ed. New York: Continuum.

Hult, C., and T. Huckin. 1999. *The New Century Handbook*. Boston: Allyn & Bacon.

Morenberg, M., J. Sommers, D. A. Daiker, and A. Kerek. 2002. *The Writer's Options: Lessons in Style and Arrangement*. 7th ed. New York: Longman.

Pirsig, R. 1974. *Zen and the Art of Motorcycle Maintenance*. 10th ed. New York: William Morrow.

Raimes, A. 1999. *Keys for Writers: A Brief Handbook*. New York: Houghton Mifflin.

Rosen, L., and L. Behrens. 1997. *The Allyn and Bacon Handbook*. 3d ed. Boston: Allyn & Bacon.

2

What Line? I Didn't See Any Line

Molly Wingate

It can happen in the middle of a tutoring session—maybe at the end. The pleasant exhilaration of working well with a writer is replaced by a queasy, uneasy sense that this session is not going so well after all. You may notice that the writer is relying on you, waiting for you to do or say something. Or you may notice that the writer has disengaged from the tutoring process, waiting for you to stop doing and saying. Either way, the session is no longer productive, and the weight of it is on your shoulders. When did the shift occur? When did this session slip over the line between being writer-centered, process-oriented, and effective to being tutor-centered, product-oriented, and fairly useless? How could you, an experienced tutor, have missed the crossing? Where is that line? How do you find it? What to do when you have crossed it? These are the guiding questions of this chapter.

Some Background

Most tutor training texts begin their conversations about tutors and their roles with the assumption that the job of a writing center is to "produce better writers, not better writing."[1] Of course, we do not have to sacrifice better writers for better writing or vice versa. Toni-Lee Capossela points out, "It's possible to make better *writers* AND better writing, but not if the writing is made better by another hand."[2] For a tutoring session to be considered productive, it is essential that the writer does the bulk of the work and learns something that can be used in future writing projects. As tutors, we know what our goals are, but sometimes it is hard to see the line between only demonstrating to the writer what could be done with a paper and teaching the writer to do those things on her own.

Figuring out how much help to give "can be personally troubling," as Christina Murphy and Steve Sherwood note. "The natural tendency to be helpful and supportive may conflict with a sense that doing too much of the student's work will not produce the desired result."[3] Here are their suggestions for how to proceed in a session:

- Give a candid opinion of the strengths and weaknesses of the work in progress; in the process, be sensitive to the student's reactions.
- Suggest ways to enhance the strengths and minimize the weaknesses in the student's writing.
- Recognize that every text and every writer is a work in progress.[4]

These suggestions can help a tutor negotiate the territory between helping and hindering.

In addition to guidelines for proceeding in a session, many tutor trainers discuss the roles that tutors can play, or as Leigh Ryan puts it, the hats that tutors wear—the ally, the coach, the commentator, the collaborator, the writing "expert," and the counselor.[5] Each of these roles is rich with possibility, just as each is fraught with potential line crossings. The tutor's task is to combine the suggestions for proceeding in a session with the roles the tutor can play to create and maintain a tutorial that stays on safe ground and helps the writer. I have been tutoring writers in writing centers since 1981, and I still struggle mightily to create and maintain this balance.

What to Do

In staff meetings at the writing center at Colorado College, we talk about sessions where the struggle didn't turn out so well. In the beginning, tutors learn to spot when they have or are just about to cross the line in the most obvious situations. If a writer asks a tutor to proofread or edit the paper, we explain why we would rather teach proofreading. When writers try to pump us for information about the paper's topic, we can tell them in all honesty that we do not have the information they seek. And although plagiarism has many nuances, we have lots of tricks to subvert the writers who would love to copy down our every word. We can give them a variety of choices, give examples that are parallel but not appropriate for the paper, or give suggestions faster than anyone could possibly write. Once we have tutored for a while, these obvious situations are predictable, and we have quick, graceful, and face-saving ways to respond. We know that every writer and every situation calls for a different approach, and we know how to improvise within a set of guidelines.

Brainstorming Sessions

The line becomes obscure when the tutorial session is focused on the ideas of a writing project. A tutor can begin to wonder whose ideas make up the paper that comes out of a session. This more subtle form of line crossing comes up often in staff meetings but has few pat responses. Take the situation of helping a student who has trouble extending ideas. Perhaps the tutor shows the writer a brainstorming heuristic that generates a lot of material. The tutor then joins in the fun of debating both sides of an issue and helps the writer answer the who, what, when, where, and how of a topic. The writer comes out of the session with a great deal more material, and it seems genuinely insightful. Coming up with critical material for the paper was the purpose of the session, but the tutor wonders whose work it was. Did the tutor collaborate or commandeer? The same question can arise when a tutor suggests a tool for analyzing a draft that results in a radical reorganization, vastly improving the paper. While the tutor and the writer are no doubt happy that the paper is improved, who did the reorganizing and did the writer learn anything about being a better writer?

When a session is focused on the ideas of a paper, tutors can lose track of their role and step over the line. Many tutors talk about how they suddenly realized that they were doing all the work in a session, that the writer hadn't talked as much as they had, or that the writer did not look or sound confident. They realized that they were no longer teaching the writer something to use in the future because they had become too involved in dazzling the writer with the possibilities they saw in the paper. The writer, along with the tutor's role as teacher, had been left behind as the tutor pushed onward toward a better paper, not a better writer. These sessions were no longer effective.

The Over *Sessions*

There is yet another category of tutors crossing the line that creates unproductive sessions. I call them the *over* sessions: overempathizing, overwhelming, and overtaking. In staff meetings when we talk about problem sessions, tutors find the over sessions the most troubling because they aren't sure when they crossed the line into unproductive territory or whether they could have avoided it. The tutor sees that a writer is quite distressed with a professor, for example, so the tutor decides to listen, even sharing experiences with similar teachers. The writer goes on to give a history of every experience of writer's block since third grade. The tutor feels sure that the writer needs to talk about these blocks to get started. The writing project is forgotten, the session is almost over, the paper is barely begun.

By *overempathizing,* tutors can make it hard for a session to be productive. In the previous example, the tutor assumes that the writer needs to talk before he can start writing—probably a safe assumption. But when sharing experiences did not move the session along to the current project, the tutor should have changed direction. Talking about past writer's blocks did not help the writer overcome them, while writing something might have. The tutor got too involved in the writer's history (a counselor's job) and lost track of the reason the writer came in—to work on a specific project.

Overwhelming a writer is the second category of unproductive over sessions. Here, the tutor, trying to be thorough, gives the writer too much information to process. The writer wants to thoroughly revise a fifteen-page paper. As the writer reads the paper, the tutor stops to point out sentence-level concerns in every other sentence. With the tutor's help, the writer revises passive voice, repairs focus problems, sorts out commas, and corrects citations. After thirty minutes, the writer's voice has gone flat. The writer stops reading, looks up wearily, and thanks the tutor for the time. "I will finish it on my own." The tutor buried the writer in too much information. Instead of picking just a few things to talk about, the tutor left the writer with the impression that there was just too much to do in the paper. With so much advice, the writer grew disheartened, and the session flopped.

On occasion, tutors cross the line by *taking over* a session. For example, a writer wishes to turn a paper on Anasazi archeological sites in the Four Corners area into a proposal for an independent study. The tutor finds this to be an interesting prospect and is genuinely curious about the Anasazi. What might otherwise seem like a perfect setup for a great session becomes unproductive as the tutor makes the project too much her own. Lines like, "Let me see if I can figure this out," "What do you think of rearranging this section like this?" and "I like this word better, don't you?" reveal that the tutor is fully engaged in her own thinking about the writing project. The writer withdraws a bit and lets the tutor do the work. The writer might be happy with the well-constructed and well-edited result of such a session but he did not learn more about becoming a good writer. In terms of tutoring, the session was unproductive.

There are several ways to cross the line between a productive tutorial where the writer learns about drafting, revising, editing, or some combination of the three, and an unproductive session where the writer gains little to carry into the next writing project. What can a tutor do to recognize the line and return to a productive session?

Getting Back on Safe Ground

My rule of thumb is this: If you think you have stepped over the line, you probably have. When a tutor senses that the session is not going as well as it might, the tutor should reevaluate his role in the session. Hallmarks of having overstepped the tutor role include talking more than the writer, noticing that the writer appears distracted or uninterested, and finding that the writer is always choosing the tutor's suggestions. Or, you know you've overstepped if you feel tired at the end of the session while the writer looks refreshed. Body language gives clues, too. If the writer is not leaning in toward the paper, then she is probably not engaged. Eye contact is another sign. As you look into the writer's eyes, do you see boredom, frustration, anger? The crossed line may be clear from across the room at this point.

Having crossed into unproductivity, tutors can get themselves back on track. First they must stop whatever it is that has made the session unproductive. Quit talking, listening, doing, or suggesting in the way that is problematic.

A tutor can even remark on this change. "Gee, I seem to have gotten carried away," "You know, I forgot to ask you to make these changes. Please look at the next sentence," or "Let's get to the business of the paper, okay?" Experience teaches tutors that it is possible to recover from line crossings and to move on.

To recover from overempathizing, tutors must remember that counseling is not their major role. Some tutors, especially those trained to work in residence halls, are better equipped than others to talk about personal problems and to know when they are in past their depth. Writing tutors generally do not have such training. Even if it seems a little rude, writing tutors must disclaim any ability to counsel. Although, as Muriel Harris points out (see Chapter 4), tutors can benefit from learning to use some of the conversational strategies that professional counselors use. A tutor can suggest some of the resources available on campus for stress management, study skills training, and so on. The writing center director can also provide guidance, especially when the tutor is concerned for the writer's well-being.

For tutors who might be concerned about overwhelming a writer or taking over a session, a technique suggested and used by a peer tutor at Colorado College can help. At the end of every paragraph or so, Amy Weible asks the writer how he feels about the changes they have made. This creates opportunities to change course in case the writer is uneasy with the progress of the session. Asking the writer about his feelings also helps to remind the tutor whose paper it is and who should be setting the pace and direction of the session. Especially whenever I feel a writer withdraw from the activity of the session, I ask, "Is this what you want to be doing?" or "Is this what you had in mind for your paper?" Writers sometimes apologize for thinking about something else or explain that they really do not have the energy for a full-scale, sentence-by-sentence revision after all. Instead of continuing on my path and taking over the session or overwhelming the writer, I can easily redirect my energies and follow the writer's lead. The session can return to being productive.

Complicating Matters

While the advice I offer works in the cases I cited, experienced tutors know that no two sessions are alike. The safe ground of one session is quicksand in another. Some writers delight in having a real person to talk with about their ideas. They have formed their own opinions and are unlikely to be easily swayed by anyone's suggestions. They carefully consider each change to a paper, making sure it is their own change. How different from the writer who is thrown into a tizzy when a tutor starts asking questions about the assumptions of a project or even to have technical jargon explained. The writer is no longer sure of anything about his paper. The writer takes every question about content to be a weakness with the paper. The tutor must be alert to the writer's reactions to the session.

It is not exactly reassuring to realize that the line always moves and that tutors find it by crossing it. Tutors have to take chances, however. Being too cautious results in sessions that are dull and unproductive. Writers come to the writing center to move their projects along; what a shame to lose them because the tutors try too hard to stay on safe ground. Tutors should not worry about taking chances or making mistakes; we are human, after all. It is normal for someone interested in writing to get excited about ideas. I encourage tutors in our writing center to give themselves a warning when they get really excited about someone else's writing project. Observe the writer's reactions and watch out for the line. Although undoubtedly everyone will misstep a bit, everyone can recover.

As writing centers learn to respond to the needs of international and ethnically diverse populations, cross-cultural tutorials can be occasions for plenty of missteps. Some of the advice offered in this chapter may take you in the wrong direction when there are cross-cultural misunderstandings at work. This most welcome complication reminds us how important it is for tutors to explain their roles and to ask writers about their expectations for the session. As a writing center director, I'm reminded to include multicultural training in tutor preparation courses, particularly training in recognizing and putting aside generalizations about national and ethnic groups.[6] Each writer is different, each session is new.

Faculty members can add another layer of complication when it comes to crossing the line, especially if they are unaware of the philosophy that informs most tutoring programs. They may be uneasy about the relationship between tutors and writers, concerned about the roles that tutors play and how they help writers, and for reasons discussed earlier, unsure about whose work is being handed in for a grade.[7] Tutoring programs gain the trust of faculty members with productive sessions that are writer- and process-centered. Not crossing the line egregiously maintains that important trust. Without assignments from the faculty, few student writers would have the occasion or the motivation to seek out the writing center. Without support from faculty members, tutoring programs can wither. If tutors routinely cross the line without returning to safe ground, they risk losing the trust of faculty and undermining the entire tutoring program. Luckily, tutors do not routinely cross the line and writing centers work hard to communicate with faculty members.

All these complicating matters have at their base the ideas of collaboration, ethics, and power. As Irene Clark puts it, "In writing labs and centers, . . . the kinds of assistance, which occurs regularly among colleagues, might raise questions, if not eyebrows, over issues of ethics."[8] The academy places different standards of acceptable collaboration on teachers, colleagues, tutors, and classmates. When an individual plays two or three of these roles, working with writers gets complicated. Debating whether these different standards are fair or even useful is a valuable part of any tutor's training. The debate hinges on questions of authority and power. For tutors, the questions about a particular session are many. Did the session diminish the writer's authority? Did the writer make all the decisions about the paper? Who directed the session? Who was in charge of the agenda? Was it a productive session? Did the writer learn something about writing that can be used in the next writing project? (See Chapter 3.) These perennial questions are at the base of any tutoring program. The answers point to how productive a session—and how successful a tutoring program—you have co-created.

Further Reading

Clark, Irene Lurkis. 1988. "Collaboration and Ethics in Writing Center Pedagogy." *Writing Center Journal* 9 (1): 3–12.

Clark discusses the many ethical concerns that have arisen around writing center tutoring, especially plagiarism. While agreeing that tutors should never do the bulk of the work, Clark points out that there are occasions when proofreading and editing can be instructive and ethical. She argues that tutors must be encouraged to be flexible about the help they provide writers.

Severino, Carol. 1992. "Rhetorically Analyzing Collaboration(s)." *Writing Center Journal* 13 (1): 53–64.

Severino provides a set of situational and interpersonal features to look at when analyzing the dynamics of a peer tutoring session. She then analyzes tutorial sessions using these features determining "how much a peer and how much a tutor a peer tutor is." Among other things, such analysis helps tutors determine when to shift between a directive/hierarchical mode and a nondirective/dialogic mode.

Sherwood, Steve. 1995. "The Dark Side of the Helping Personality: Student Dependency and the Potential for Tutor Burnout." In *Writing Center Perspectives,* eds. B. Stay, C. Murphy, and E. Hobson, 63–70. Emmitsburg, MD: National Writing Centers Association Press.

As the title suggests, Sherwood looks at when a tutor's tendency to be helpful can cause real trouble. He lists symptoms of neurotic unselfishness that lead to creating student dependency and other problems for writing centers and the profession. He suggests using detached concern to correct for this martyr complex gone awry.

Notes

1. Stephen North, "The Idea of a Writing Center," *College English* 46 (1984): 438.
2. Toni-Lee Capossela, *The Harcourt Brace Guide to Peer Tutoring* (Fort Worth, TX: Harcourt Brace College, 1998), 2. Emphasis in original.
3. Christina Murphy and Steve Sherwood, *The St. Martin's Sourcebook for Writing Tutors* (New York: St. Martin's, 1995), 13.
4. Murphy and Sherwood, 15.
5. Leigh Ryan, *The Bedford Guide for Writing Tutors* (Boston: St. Martin's, 1994), 23–24.

6. Peter Mulvihill, Keith Nitta, and Molly Wingate, "Into the Fray: Ethnicity and Tutor Preparation," *Writing Lab Newsletter* 19 (7) (1995): 2.

7. For an example of this, see Steve Sherwood, "Ethics and Improvisation," *Writing Lab Newsletter* 22 (4) (1997): 1.

8. Irene Lurkis Clark, "Collaboration and Ethics in Writing Center Pedagogy," *Writing Center Journal* 9 (1) (1988): 3.

Works Cited

Capossela, T. 1998. *The Harcourt Brace Guide to Peer Tutoring.* Fort Worth, TX: Harcourt Brace College.

Clark, I. L. 1988. "Collaboration and Ethics in Writing Center Pedagogy." *Writing Center Journal* 9 (1): 3–12.

Mulvihill, P., K. Nitta, and M. Wingate. 1995. "Into the Fray: Ethnicity and Tutor Preparation." *Writing Lab Newsletter* 19 (7): 1–5.

Murphy, C., and S. Sherwood. 1995. *The St. Martin's Sourcebook for Writing Tutors.* New York: St. Martin's.

North, S. 1984. "The Idea of a Writing Center." *College English* 46: 433–46.

Ryan, L. 1994. *The Bedford Guide for Writing Tutors.* Boston: St. Martin's.

Sherwood, S. 1997. "Ethics and Improvisation." *Writing Lab Newsletter* 22 (4): 1–5.

3

(Non)Meeting of the Minds

A Study in Frustration

Nicole Kraemer Munday

Why do we need to study the dynamics of tutoring? Often a session goes well and it is easy to see how and why the writer benefited. Sometimes, however, both the tutor and the writer leave disappointed. What went wrong? That's often hard to figure out—an unfortunate thing because the stakes can be high. For the writer, a tutoring session may be the first time in her life when anyone has given more than a few minutes of undivided attention to her writing. Or it may be that success on this particular assignment is important to her in ways no one but the student will ever know. For the tutor, the session may represent the most thoughtful and skilled approach she is capable of. Or it may be an attempt at necessary and constructive criticism of a paper whose writer wants none of it.

As with any social interaction, a tutoring session always retains a hint of mystery because the true motivations and feelings of each participant are seldom explicitly stated. Tutors and writers can only guess at these based on the verbal and nonverbal feedback they receive. Taking on the role of a voyeur can help us interpret this feedback in a more careful and deliberate way. It can help us understand why some sessions seem to go so smoothly, while others appear more turbulent.

Perhaps you have had the opportunity to observe a session in person. If so, you have probably noticed that it's like a minidrama, with an unfolding conversation, changing facial expressions, expressive body language, a struggle for understanding, the relief of accomplishment, and hopefully, a happy ending. While reading the narrative of a session is not the same as seeing one in real life, it has the benefit of slowing down the interaction so that you can examine it and imagine how the outcome of the session was affected by the steps that led up to it.

The following narrative provides an opportunity to observe a tutoring session and then discuss it with your fellow tutors. As you read the narrative, try the following:

- Put yourself in the tutor's seat and then the writer's. How does this change the way you understand the session?
- Imagine how you would have handled the session if you were the tutor.

It's a rainy Monday morning when Portia strides into the writing center, prompt for her appointment. She has a no-nonsense, efficient demeanor as she checks in at the front desk, holding a checklist for the session on top of her pile of books. This is not your typical first-year visitor to the writing center—timid, fumbling, unsure whether to stand or sit. Portia is a fourth-year English major who works part-time at the public library to help pay for college, and the good grades she receives make her hard work in and out of the classroom seem worthwhile. She is a highly organized student who likes to begin assignments several weeks before they are due. Portia receives mostly Bs on her essays but usually manages to get As and Bs in her classes. She has hopes of going to graduate school and knows that writing well will be even more important there.

A second-year tutor, Sally works ten hours per week in the writing center and is highly regarded by other members of the staff for her intelligence and good nature; overall, she receives very positive evaluations for her tutoring. She is plain-spoken and has a knack for saying what other people are thinking but are reluctant to express.

Sally has done some reading in the field of writing center theory and she knows that the debate over whether it is better to be a nondirective or directive tutor remains unresolved. Both approaches have their supporters and detractors. The nondirective approach puts the writer in control, relies more on the writer's involvement, and usually takes longer. The directive approach is arguably more frank and straightforward. It can take less time, and it is often what students expect. Sally, familiar with both sides of the debate, has decided that what students want is what benefits them most—and it is also the tutoring style with which she is most comfortable. So, she tells students what she knows and thinks, and from there writers are free to make up their own minds. Besides, she says that being nondirective makes her seem "fakey," and that doesn't suit her. Her approach is to tell students what she thinks—politely but frankly.

When Sally calls Portia's name and they exchange greetings, Portia chooses a table near the wall and they soon settle in.

Portia: My paper is due tomorrow, and I've never been here before . . . but I figured maybe I should have somebody look at it before I turn it in. It's finished, basically.

Sally: Okay, well here in the writing center we . . .

Portia [Interrupting]: Have you ever heard of Kiefer? This is the first time I've had a class with her. Have you had her before?

Sally [Shakes her head]: I'm an international studies major, so . . .

Portia: Oh. Well, she grades hard. My paper's about Frost's poems—Robert Frost? [*Sally nods*]—and connecting with other people and being open and sincere about it.

Sally: So you're writing an analysis . . .

Portia: Yeah, a lit analysis paper, which I've written a ton of already, but like I said, the grading in this class is ridiculous, and I guess I don't give her what she wants.

Sally: Okay. Well, let's look at your paper and see what you've got.

Portia: Wait. [*Places assignment on the table*] Dr. Kiefer gave us an assignment with a list of things to do in our papers. I don't know if this is going to make sense to you since you're not an English major.

Sally: Well, let's see. [*Reads the assignment and list*]

Portia: Maybe you could just check to make sure my commas are good and that my intro is catchy enough.

Sally: I don't see those things listed here, but one of the items on your list is diction and it's circled. Does that mean . . . ?

Portia: . . . she doesn't like my writing style. Ya know, sometimes I feel like throwing this paper out the window.

Sally: Don't do that . . . I'd have to call campus police on you—for littering! [*Portia is not amused*] Let's do this. Go ahead and read it to me and then we'll talk about the whole paper and the best way to . . .

Portia: You want me to *read* it to you? Out loud?

So far, Portia feels this session is not helping her. She has asked for help with commas and the introduction because she doesn't feel that an international studies major really knows how to address problems with a paper in a senior-level English course, and she doesn't want to waste a lot of time. Sally, meanwhile, never got a chance to give her opening speech on what-to-expect-from-the-writing-center, and she has struggled to figure out how best to help Portia. When she saw *diction* circled on the assignment, she asked Portia about it, but that's when she noticed that Portia's attitude headed south. Hoping to put the session back on an even keel, Sally asked Portia to read the paper aloud, but now thinks this was a mistake, too. Portia decides to go along and she reads it, reluctantly:

> For poet Robert Frost—a genius who encaptivated the hearts and minds of his readers—practiced restraint is an important and vital part of human relationships. If a person exhibits restraint, they have slowed down long enough to think about the best way to have a meeting of the minds with

another person or people. Too often, humans fill their lives with "turning to fresh tasks" ("Wood-Pile" 35) or chasing after some "final goal" ("On a Tree Fallen Across the Road" 10), instead of caring for one another. Unfortunately, when people start to ignore one another, friendships wither like the faded beauty of wilted rose blooms. The bottom line is—people need to walk a fine line between giving each other space and being there for one another.

Basically, there are three surmountable attitudes one can have when it comes to reacting to others—reckless abandon, avoidance, or restraint. Reckless abandon means showing intense emotion—whether it is joy, anger, or grief. People who give themselves up to reckless abandon really cannot seem to control themselves—they may appear to others as off their rocker or as off the wall. Their behavior actually could be a conscious decision because they do not want to take responsibility for thinking about their actions—or maybe they have not given the situation any thought at all and have fallen into reckless abandon because they just never really stopped to figure out the right way to act.

When Portia reaches the bottom of the first page, she sighs and rolls her eyes. They are about fifteen minutes into a forty-minute session, and Sally decides it's a good time to stop and sort things out.

Sally: Okay, that was really helpful to me, to hear you read the beginning of your paper so I could hear what it's about. I think we need to decide what's the best way to spend the time we have left. The paper is due tomorrow morning, right? You mentioned commas and your introduction—is that still what you want to work on? [*Portia stares blankly*]

Sally: What about diction?

Portia: I think my interpretation is good.

Sally: I totally agree. What do you think about the way you present yourself . . . you know, your tone?

Portia: What do you mean?

Sally: Like when you talk about friendships withering like "wilted rose blooms" . . . that's kind of flowery, you know? No pun intended. [*Smiles*]

Portia: I think you're missing the point. That's just some description I used to pull in my readers, to paint a picture for them.

Sally [*Sits up in her chair*]: Okay, but this is a literary analysis paper. Sometimes it's good to take a step backward and take a more neutral or objective tone. It's not like you're trying to write poetry here, you're wanting to *analyze* it.

Portia: Hmmm. . . . What else?

Sally: Okay. Here are some other spots. In the second paragraph, where you say "off their rocker or off the wall." The language is really informal. Is your professor okay with informal writing like this, or . . . ?

Portia [Slides her paper across the table closer toward herself]: You know, I'm just not seeing what the big problem is. All my teachers tell me how they love the way I write. I try to be more creative than other students.

Sally: Creativity is great. But some of these clichés don't come across as creative, to me at least.

[*Portia says nothing, but gives Sally a hard, icy stare*]

Sally: Look, I just want to point out some things that I noticed when you read me your paper, some things that I think might relate to your assignment. Then, you can decide whether you want to change them or not. It's totally up to you.

Portia [Slowly]: Right.

Sally: Another thing is, I see a lot of dashes. It's okay to use them sometimes, but when they're overused they lose their effect. So if this diction thing is important, I'd say you should work on editing for things like that, and extra words, redundancies, clutter. Maybe just take the clutter out.

Portia: Anything else?

Sally: Well, we've got about five minutes or so left. What would you like to do?

Portia: I don't know, but I've got to go now. [*Portia starts packing up to leave*] Thanks. I'll work on this some more.

When Sally rehashed the session with a fellow tutor, she said she was distressed that her interaction with Portia had been so tense. Sally explained, "For me, the personal relationship between me and the writers is the most rewarding part of working here. But I can't tell people everything is fine when I believe they need to do more work on their papers. I couldn't develop any kind of rapport with her, and I'm not sure she wanted to develop any with me."

One way to look at this scenario is in terms of mismatched expectations. Over time, Sally had developed a routine way to open each session, one where she carefully explained what writers could expect during their time at the writing center. Sally expected first-time visitors, such as Portia, to listen attentively to her spiel. But Portia's take-charge attitude and preprepared tutoring agenda caught Sally off guard. At the same time, Portia figured writing center tutors would operate the same way the reference librarians did where she worked. She thought she'd sit down, she'd tell the tutor what kind of feedback she needed, and then she'd leave as a satisfied customer. Portia did not expect Sally to challenge her to think about her paper in a substantive way; she was looking for validation as a writer and perhaps a few minor proofreading tips. How could their mismatched expectations have been reconciled? Were their goals for the session so incompatible that their impasse was inevitable, or was there a way for each of them to articulate their objectives more candidly?

Interpersonal interaction offers another lens through which we can see this session. We can analyze Portia's and Sally's nonverbal clues to understand significant turning points and missed opportunities during the session. For example, in the beginning, Portia interrupts Sally several times. Does Portia do this because she is trying to establish dominance during the session or because she is working to maintain authorial control? Is she interrupting because she is especially anxious about her assignment or because she is uneasy about visiting the writing center for the first time? Whether Portia's interruptions come out of impoliteness, fear, or something else altogether is a critical question— each possibility begs for a different response from Sally.

Also, if it is as important to Sally as she says it is to establish a rapport with writers, did she do enough to call attention to what Portia did *right* in her essay? The old adage about attracting more flies with honey than with vinegar still applies (as does Mary Poppin's tip that "just a spoonful of sugar helps the medicine go down"). Most writers want to hear their work praised, as well as criticized, and fortunately there were a number of legitimate strengths in the paper that Sally could have mentioned. For example, Portia defines her terms nicely at the start of her essay, she explains the relevance of the poetry lines she cites, and she uses punctuation correctly and in a sophisticated way (despite her being overly enamored with em dashes). Did Sally recognize these qualities in Portia's writing or was Sally blinded to them because she felt defensive and threatened?

Writing center sessions are dynamic and unpredictable events. Like a theatrical production, at any moment the plot can take a hairpin turn, leading writers and tutors to unexpected revelations or disastrous endings. There's one major difference, though, between the theater and the writing center: in real-time sessions, there is no script.

Further Reading

Clark, Irene L., and Dave Healy. 2001. "Are Writing Centers Ethical?" In *The Allyn and Bacon Guide to Writing Center Theory and Practice*, eds. Robert W. Barnett and Jacob S. Blumner, 242–59. Boston: Allyn & Bacon. Reprinted from *WPA: Writing Program Administration* (1996).

Shamoon, Linda K., and Deborah H. Burns. 1995. "A Critique of Pure Tutoring." *Writing Center Journal* 15 (2): 134–51.

Together, these two articles offer tutors some good insights into the debate over directive versus nondirective tutoring, and they add a new perspective to the session with Portia and Sally. These articles show that choosing one approach or the other is not a simple matter.

4

Talk to Me

Engaging Reluctant Writers

Muriel Harris

Every tutor, no matter how dazzlingly effective he is, will meet up with a student who responds—or fails to respond—like the one in this all-too-familiar dialogue:

Tutor: Hi, Alisa, how are you doin' today?

Alisa: [*Nods silently and briefly, begins searching in her backpack for her paper, and then settles far back into her seat, hands in her lap*]

Tutor: Were you at the game this weekend? I knew we were going to lose, but it was a good game to watch.

Alisa: [*Shakes her head slightly, to indicate she didn't go*]

Tutor: Well, what do you want to work on today?

Alisa: Here's my paper. [*She looks down, avoiding eye contact*]

Tutor: Why don't you tell me a bit about it. . . . What your main point is, what the assignment is . . . you know, all that stuff that we'll need to know to work on it.

Alisa: It's about cloning. For my Ethics class. It's due in a couple of days.

Tutor: OK, interesting subject. That's a hot topic, and there's lots to say about it. What do you want to work on?

Alisa: Could you see if it's OK?

Tutor: OK, let's start with the main point. Why don't you just tell me first what your main point is. [*Waits while the silence grows and expands around them*] Is cloning ethical? Are there ethical problems we should consider before going ahead? Should scientists try to do it?

Alisa: It's OK, I guess.

Tutor: Are you supposed to discuss the ethical implications? Or argue a point of view? Are you writing to people who think cloning should be stopped? Or to people who think it's important to do, like for possible medical uses?

Alisa: It really doesn't much affect me. I don't know. [*Alisa shrugs, slumps farther down in her chair, and stares at the people at the next tutorial table*]

Tutor: Did you have a hard time writing this paper? If so, let's talk about that for a bit.

Alisa: [*No response*]

And so it goes with the unresponsive student. You try to coax, nudge, or invite the student to get involved in a discussion about the paper. But the student resists and continues to sit there refusing to make eye contact or lean closer to the table. Nothing seems to engage the writer into the conversation you'd like to have about that paper lying limp and forlorn on the table between you and the student. You recognize the student's sense of being withdrawn from the tutorial by the student's body language, voice tone, the long silences that meet your attempts to chat, the monosyllables that pass as answers, and the shrugs that follow.

Some Background

The reasons for a student's unresponsive behavior range widely, and clues as to why a student is not responding to the tutor's efforts are usually inadequate. Some possibilities to consider:

The student is forced to be there.

When we are required to do something, some people react negatively. They may blame whoever required their attendance or whomever they meet in the process of fulfilling what was required of them. Psychologists who prepare therapists and counselors explain that it's not unusual for clients to become angry at whomever they have to meet with, even if that person is not involved in setting the requirement. Similarly, when an unwilling student is assigned to come to the writing center, the student is likely to resist a tutor's overtures to engage in any conversation. She doesn't want to be there and hopes to be able to leave as soon as possible.

Writing is not important to this writer.

Writing is seen by some students (usually mistakenly, but they don't learn this until they graduate and have to communicate on the job) as a requirement that has little to do with their lives. They envision themselves as engineers in design labs, as programmers of the next generation of cool software, as pharmacists or farmers who will be far from the world of reports and memos. They assume that the business world proceeds via cell phones, not written memos or letters (which, if needed, secretaries will clean up). And, finally, they see no need for a tutor's help with writing any more than they would attend closely to someone explaining how to build mud huts. It's simply not relevant to their lives, and they most likely came to the writing center because it was required, because they thought they'd earn extra points with the teacher, or because they want the tutor to fix the paper so they can get a higher grade.

The writer may be anxious about revealing ignorance or poor writing to anyone and nervous about being critiqued.

For a study I conducted to learn about students' concerns in writing tutorials ("Talking in the Middle"), I read hundreds of student responses on anonymous evaluations filled out at the end of tutorials in our Writing Lab. Over and over, they commented how relieved they were that they weren't "slammed" or "laughed at" or "ripped" by the tutor. They were surprised that the tutor didn't talk down to them. They announced that the tutorial was successful because they now felt more confident, though it was usually not clear if they meant more confident about themselves or their writing—or perhaps both. From comments like these, we become more aware of how apprehensive students are when they come to writing centers. Under such emotional strains, they may be very likely to shut up, to wonder what they're supposed to do, and finally, to be as unengaged as any tutor might be in a strange situation. When we have no idea what's expected of us and we feel shaky about whether we are going to be ridiculed or asked to demonstrate what we don't know, we do sometimes respond by withdrawing until we can get a better handle on what's happening or figure out how we can retreat from the situation with minimal embarrassment.

The student is overwhelmed by other concerns.

The student who doesn't want to engage in tutorial conversation may have just heard that he's running out of financial aid, that there was a major quiz in the chem lecture he missed, or that his girlfriend has dumped him. Students bring with them a variety of other problems and worries and disappointments that affect their ability (or inability) to attend to what's going on in the writing tutorial. Issues that can affect students' writing are categorized by Leigh Ryan as academic (grades, study skills, test anxiety), social (separation from family and friends, peer pressure, roommates), and lifestyle (finances, independence, job responsibilities).[1]

The writer doesn't have the language to talk about her writing.

Researchers on cognitive processes involved in writing and revising (Flower et al. 1986) have explained that like other problem-solving tasks, effective revision requires the ability to detect problems in the draft of a paper and to find strategies to use to solve those problems. Without such abilities, which are often lacking in beginning writers, they don't know how to explain to someone else what they want to work on or what their problem is. Such students are likely to come in flustered, ill-at-ease, and unable to say more than "my paper's too short," "the paper doesn't flow," or "I just don't like it," or "it's not what I wanted to say" and hope that the tutor somehow understands what they mean. They lapse into silence because they don't know what to say or how to say it. Like the patient in a doctor's office, they hope that by sitting quietly while the doctor examines them, the doctor will diagnose their problem and prescribe a treatment.

The writer is simply a very quiet person.

Much research on personality type has helped us to define personality preferences, those ways of interacting with the world that are neither right nor wrong, simply ways that people differ. The Myers-Briggs Type Indicator (MBTI), one of the most useful and most well-researched ways to sort out personality preferences, has stimulated a great deal of research on how personality types interact with writing and tutoring. A particularly helpful collection of essays about this is Thomas C. Thompson's *Most Excellent Differences: Essays in Using Type Theory in the Composition Classroom* (1996). In the introduction to type theory, Thompson defines one of the MBTI dimensions as Extraversion and Introversion, noting that introverts prefer to "play out potential actions mentally before deciding whether they actually wanted to follow through with them."[2] A further picture of how introverts prefer to deal with the world shows us how we might interpret their unresponsiveness as not being engaged when, in fact, they are simply taking things in to reflect on them quietly—on their own at a later time. Here's Thompson's picture:

> Because [introverts] like to rehearse their answers before speaking, they may be slow to respond to questions about new material. Introverts often choose to sit near the edge of the classroom, where they can observe class activities without being caught in the middle of them.[3]

And, of course, some people are just naturally shy or quiet, not given to a lot of chatter. Some of us love to pour out words; others use them sparingly. Some find silence in a conversation awkward; others appreciate it as time for reflection.

The student knows that if she shuts up, the tutor (or teacher) will do all the work.

Some students who have been in school for a number of years learn how to play the teacher/tutor game to their advantage. In lectures, large classrooms, and even small ones, they've learned that they are expected to shut up, be passive, and wait for the teacher to answer her own questions. This role is all too familiar. Less familiar is the one that tutors are trying to get students to play— to be active learners who take charge of their own learning. So they wait for the tutors to tell them what to write, how to fix the paper, or maybe—if they sit quietly long enough—even do the rewriting.

What to Do

While it's not always clear which of the possibilities just listed looms largest in keeping the student withdrawn from the situation, here are some strategies to try:

Empathize about being forced to do something.

When you ask the student if her visit is required and she indicates morosely that she's there because she has to be and her actions indicate that she has no interest in doing anything much beyond sitting there until the time is up and she can leave, you can try talking openly and honestly about her not wanting to be there. Empathize, let her know that you too have been in situations you were forced into and that you too felt as she does. After all, it isn't the worst trait in the world to be an independent person who isn't exactly pleased when others tell her what to do. Try to help the student see that as long as she's bothered to come to the lab, you'd like to help her make good use of her time. If your center sends notes to teachers, explain—after you've managed to get the student to see that you are interested in her welfare—that you have to report on what was worked on and if nothing was talked about, the teacher isn't likely to consider the requirement fulfilled. Have the student help you write the note (or let her write it herself). If none of this mobilizes the student into some minimal conversation, you have probably done what you could. You need to let the student leave, but you've warned her (in friendly terms) that sitting there won't satisfy the instructor. Just as we encourage students to make their own decisions about what they want to write, letting them make the decision to leave without really satisfying the requirement at least keeps students in the driver's seat. Some tutors find that these students return later, on their own, when it's not required and after they've realized that tutors aren't there to force them to do anything.

Acknowledge the lack of interest in writing and try for a small success.

For writers who admit that they have little interest in writing and say that it isn't relevant to them, you can start by acknowledging this attitude as something many students share. But then try talking about when the student might need writing skills—in classes (exams, reports) or for that person's career (job applications, memos). Harold Hackney and L. Sherilyn Cormier, in their book on how counselors can help clients, warn us that "unless clients can determine some personal goals for counseling, the probability of change is minimal."[4] You won't win over everyone because some students will remain unconvinced that being a better writer is a personal goal of theirs, and they will continue to expend as little effort as possible. Then, it's time to try for a minimal bit of success. The student has some piece of writing to work on or she wouldn't be there. What can be done with that one paper? One tutor in our Writing Lab, when backed into such corners by students who merely wanted to pass the course and not worry about writing any more, would explain that he realized the student's time was valuable and didn't want to waste it. What could they do together in the few remaining minutes of the tutorial to make it useful for the student? Sometimes that might result in little more than helping the student set up his two citations in MLA format or learn the difference between *it's* and *its*, but at least the time together was not a total waste.

Help the student talk about his fears.

If you sense the student is quiet because he is overcome by anxiety or fears of some kind related to meeting you and talking about his writing, try to establish an atmosphere of trust, perhaps by being friendly, by explaining that you're not a teacher and that your job is to help and to listen. Then invite the student to talk about his anxieties. In their suggestions to counselors who work with fearful clients, psychotherapists Randolph Pipes and Donna Davenport tell us that such clients often cannot overcome their resistance to getting involved until the underlying fears are expressed. Then, it is important to empathize and to reassure the student that such fears are not uncommon and can be overcome. The core of such a conversation might sound like this:

Tutor: You don't seem to want to talk about your paper. Would you like me to read it instead, or would that bother you? When I was in freshman comp, I hated having my paper read by anyone, especially out loud in class and in front of others. I wouldn't even let my roommate read my papers.

Writer: I'm not a good writer. My teachers hate my writing. I'll never be good at it.

Tutor: I honestly don't know a whole lot of people who think they're great writers. Writing takes work, and you probably aren't happy with what you write. That's pretty usual. And we can work on your writing together. I bet there's lots of good stuff here to work with.

Writer: I hate when someone criticizes my writing. I won't show it to anyone except my teacher.

Tutor: Hey, I'm not going to criticize. Really. My job is to help you. In fact, I like the first paragraph here, especially when you start out with that good question in your first sentence. Talking about your writing with someone else usually helps a lot.

Reschedule for a better time or listen and move on.

For students who seem withdrawn or remain unengaged because there might be other, more pressing problems on their minds, you can ask if they want to come back some other time. Or if the student starts to talk about what's worrying her, listen. Give the student a few minutes to vent or explain what's really on her mind, and really listen. Pipes and Davenport distinguish between "social listening," which is often largely a matter of not interrupting, maybe nodding from time to time, or thinking of what you're going to say next, and "therapeutic listening," which requires much more. The therapeutic listener attends closely, really hears what the client is saying and both processes cognitively what the client is saying while empathizing closely with what is being said. A few minutes of such conversation is likely to help clear the air, but if you sense that the person starts bringing up other problems, having found a listening ear, it's probably clear that the student is deciding to use the time as a support session for her life, her troubles, her frustration with her roommate. One strategy to get back to work is first to acknowledge that you've heard the student and that it's time to move on. You can show that you were listening by reflecting back to the student what she said: "Yeah, getting a speeding ticket really upsets you. But now let's focus on something positive, like getting that paper revised." Or "You sound like you're fearful about what's happening with your mom, but I'm not trained to help you with that. There's good psych services here on campus. It's free, and a couple of my friends went there and were glad they did. I can help you make an appointment. But, for now, since we only have about twenty minutes left, what can we do in that time to help you revise this paper?"

Offer the student some questions he can ask himself.

When a student can't offer much beyond general unease about the paper (not liking it, thinking it doesn't flow, etc.) and you suspect that the student is quiet because he has nothing else to say, try giving the student some possible questions to ask himself:

> "Could you tell me if part of the problem is that what you wanted to do in this paper—what's in your head—doesn't match with what's here on the page?"
> (or)
> "Do you think the lack of flow is because there aren't words to tie the sentences and paragraphs together? Or maybe you think it doesn't flow because it jumps from topic to topic? Sometimes, people get that 'lack of flow' feeling when the order is jumbled or when they're not sure whether the different parts are in some kind of logical order."
> (or)
> "Are you wondering if the paper doesn't meet the assignment? Or the kind of paper it's supposed to be, like a persuasion paper or a definition paper?"

If this helps the student to start talking, you can remind him that these are good questions to ask himself when he's working on a draft and wants to improve it. You may have to keep listing questions and problems the student's paper might have until something strikes a responsive chord. When he hears something that begins to sound right, he will begin—probably hesitantly—to talk more easily about what he wants to work on.

Give the student some quiet time to think and write.

If you meet up with a truly quiet person who has little to say, you don't have to fill the silence with talk. Let that person process what is being said and leave some quiet time for her to think about your question. Ask if she'd prefer to try writing about it herself while you work with another student, assuring her that you'll come back to continue working together. Try to set a specific task for her to work on:

Tutor: If you're having difficulties making the paper longer, why not try the journalist's questions—who, what, where, why, when, how? Maybe who's going to benefit from more student parking on campus; where such parking would be; why the administration should consider your proposal; what the administration might bring up as arguments against your proposal. Want to write down those question words to think about? I'll be back in awhile to see how you're doing, OK?

In their discussion of how to use personality preferences to work with writing, Sharon Cramer and Tom Reigstad found that for those who score highly as extraverts on the MBTI scale "an opportunity to brainstorm with fellow writers would be welcome [while] . . . individuals with the 'introverted' preference . . . would more likely benefit from independent brooding in private and would write best in a sanctuary, like a study carrel."[5]

Try minimalist tutoring.

When the writer keeps looking to you to do all the work and is willing to sit there silently and outwait you, you can try Jeff Brooks' "defensive minimalist tutoring." Drawing on his experience in tutoring such students, he recommends mimicking the student's body language. If the student slouches back in his chair, getting as far away as possible, the tutor can also physically move away, also slouching back into her chair. Jane Wilson, another tutor who has encountered such students, seconds this strategy: "If the student acts tired out and disinterested, the tutor can lay back in his chair and wait for something to happen. In this case, the pressure is now on the student to do something."[6] Even if being a defensive minimalist tutor is not your style, too over the top for you, try to ask questions that indicate you are interested in the student's answers, refrain from answering your own questions, and give the student plenty of wait time to answer. Eventually, most students get involved, at least minimally.

Complicating Matters

The strategies offered here come with a number of caveats. They may not work, but if they do, they may work in ways you don't want them to. For example, if you are successful in helping a writer talk through her fears or anxieties, she may become overly dependent on you. You begin to suspect that some of her visits to the center are mainly to talk with you as a comforting listening ear or to have you look over the paper because she has come to depend on you to approve every paper before handing it in. Then, you have to think about how to help her become independent. It's also possible that by talking to you, the writer is not seeking the kinds of professional help she ought to be getting. You can prepare for this by learning more about the professional resources on your campus. Perhaps professionals from those services can visit your staff meetings and help you to recognize symptoms. Similarly, if you are successful in turning to off-topic conversation, you may find it hard to get the student back to work. By offering an escape valve for what he doesn't want to do, you may have let him continue to avoid working on his writing. His teacher will be equally disappointed, especially if the teacher hears that he went to see a tutor and had a good discussion about changing his major. The teacher will be less likely to refer students to a place where the required work wasn't done. This is also a possible outcome when you tried and tried to get the writer to become engaged in a tutorial and finally had to let him go because he wouldn't or couldn't focus on his writing. Teachers who aren't familiar with tutorial principles and assume the tutor will take control of the session and tell the student what he needs to know will consider the tutor—and the writing center—ineffective.

It would make tutoring much easier if the strategies I've just listed came with a guarantee that they will work. They don't. Every student is a different human being, and as we all know, we all act differently at different times. Moreover, your tutoring style differs from other tutors'. You may be able to be a minimalist tutor, but you may also not find that a comfortable stance because it strikes you as rude. You may welcome students' personal conversations about their lives and problems, or you may be the kind of person for whom this is awkward. While you know that others on your staff can try these counseling strategies, you recognize that you can't. And some days you start off eager to help, and by the end of your assigned time, you really are exhausted and can't listen as closely as you know you want to. So, while strategies sound useful and easy, they aren't recipes. Sometimes the best we can hope for is a repertoire of strategies to draw on. When one doesn't seem to be working or doesn't fit the way we tutor, we move on to another one. That's what makes tutoring so challenging and finally, when we're successful, so rewarding. In the Writing Lab I work in, we agree that when you've had a bad tutorial, you should try to reflect on what went wrong and learn from it. When you conclude that part of the problem was the student and there's nothing more you can do, let it go. When you've just had a great tutorial, take a moment to just sit and enjoy the feeling.

Further Reading

Bolander, Becky, and Marcia Harrington. 1996. "Reflectivity: Finding Gold in the Crevices of Tutorials." *Writing Lab Newsletter* 20 (10): 1–5.

When a student begins to talk about other problems or frustrations in her life, and when tutors listen attentively, valuable information and insights (the gold in the crevices) about the student and her writing can emerge. Bolander and Harrington explain that such listening helps to remind us that students come to tutorials with experiences that affect their writing.

Parbst, John R. 1994. "Off-topic Conversation and the Tutoring Session." *Writing Lab Newsletter* 19 (1): 1–2, 6.

When meeting with a nervous or shy student, Parbst recommends that tutors try moving away from a tutorial agenda to off-topic conversation. This can result in relaxing the student and, as a side-benefit, may turn up ideas for writing. Possible clues that Parbst suggests for starting off-topic conversation include a student's name that might lead to conversation about the origins of the name and further conversation about the student's background; a student's athletic clothes or sport logos that may lead to questions about the upcoming sports season; or books in a student's backpack that can lead to conversations about other courses or the student's major and future plans.

Pipes, Randolph B., and Donna S. Davenport. 1990. *Introduction to Psychotherapy: Common Clinical Wisdom.* Englewood Cliffs, NJ: Prentice Hall.

Because tutors encounter similar problems that therapists or counselors meet with, this book offers suggestions for tutors as well. Topics include fears counselors have, such as the fear of looking foolish and the fear of not being competent to help; fears that clients may have that will influence how clients act; ways to start the first session; levels of listening and signals of poor listening; methods to deal with the client's resistance to help that is being offered; and so on.

Notes

1. Leigh Ryan, *The Bedford Guide for Writing Tutors,* 3d ed. (Boston: Bedford Books of St. Martin's, 2002), 51–52.
2. Thomas C. Thompson, ed., *Most Excellent Differences: Essays in Using Type Theory in the Composition Classroom* (Gainesville, FL: CAPT, 1996), 5.
3. Thompson, 6.
4. Harold L. Hackney and L. Sherilyn Cormier, *The Professional Counselor: A Process Guide to Helping,* 3d ed. (Boston: Allyn & Bacon, 1996), 117.
5. Sharon Cramer and Tom Reigstad, "Using Personality to Teach Writing," *Composition Chronicle* 7 (2) (March 1994): 4.
6. Jane C. Wilson, "Making the Sale: Helping Students to 'Buy' Writing Skills," *Writing Lab Newsletter* 21 (10) (1999): 13.

Works Cited

Brooks, J. 1991. "Minimalist Tutoring: Making the Student Do All the Work." *Writing Lab Newsletter* 15 (6): 1–4.

Cramer, S., and T. Reigstad. 1994. "Using Personality to Teach Writing." *Composition Chronicle* 7 (2) (March): 4–7.

Flower, L. R., J. R. Hayes, L. Carey, K. Schriver, and J. Stratman. 1986. "Detection, Diagnosis, and the Strategies of Revision." *College Composition and Communication* 37 (February): 16–55.

Hackney, H. L., and L. S. Cormier. 1996. *The Professional Counselor: A Process Guide to Helping*. 3d ed. Boston: Allyn & Bacon.

Harris, M. 1995. "Talking in the Middle: Why Writers Need Writing Tutors." *College English* 57 (1): 27–42.

Ryan, L. 2002. *The Bedford Guide for Writing Tutors*. 3d ed. Boston: Bedford of St. Martin's.

Thompson, T. C., ed. 1996. *Most Excellent Differences: Essays in Using Type Theory in the Composition Classroom*. Gainesville, FL: CAPT.

Wilson, J. C. 1999. "Making the Sale: Helping Students to 'Buy' Writing Skills." *Writing Lab Newsletter* 21 (10): 13–14.

5

Tutoring in Emotionally Charged Sessions

Corinne Agostinelli, Helena Poch, and Elizabeth Santoro

Since peer tutoring is an interaction between human beings, each with their own ideas and experiences, the potential for conflict is always present.[1] Perhaps the writer has chosen a subject that is particularly close to his heart, so much so that he is unable to look at the writing objectively. Or perhaps the writer has particularly strong feelings about the subject she has chosen, making it difficult or even impossible for a tutor to work objectively with the writing. Situations like these come up often enough to present real dilemmas that leave us uncertain about what to do. In this chapter we explore ways to handle emotionally charged sessions and offer different perspectives for thinking about them. As tutors, our primary responsibility is to see that the writer gets the help that he or she needs. We will focus on doing this in a respectful and productive way.

While much has been written about how to tutor, most advice deals with more practical matters such as how to ask thought-provoking questions or how to deal with time constraints. The literature about tutoring tends to focus mostly on the "brain," leaving out the "heart." However, our experiences in the writing center tell us that we need to be prepared for both aspects of tutoring. At least one book, Martha Maxwell's *When Tutor Meets Student,* informs our understanding of emotional issues by presenting a collection of stories written by writing tutors about their experiences. A few of these stories address topics such as how to handle sexist or racist writers, what to do when a personal tragedy affects a writer's ability to work, and how to build a trusting relationship between tutor and writer. Occasionally, peer tutor newsletters like *The Dangling Modifier* or *Writing Lab Newsletter* publish pieces about emotional conflict, or the topic is discussed at conferences like the National Conference on Peer Tutoring in Writing, which in 1998 was the impetus for this chapter.[2] For the most part, however, a tutor is expected to figure out the "heart" aspects of tutoring on her own. We've developed through experience our own ways of dealing with sensitive situations.

The following incident illustrates our point. A young woman's instructor gave the assignment, "Tell me about a moment in your life that says something about the rest of your life." She was having difficulty describing to her tutor what her problems with the paper were and elected, instead, to simply dive in and read the paper aloud. Two sentences into it, she choked up and began to weep. It turned out that she had chosen to write about her mother's rape as a teenager, and how hearing that story had made this young woman overly cautious and paranoid when she entered college. Her emotions had blocked her ability to work with the paper; she had, in fact, written a piece that was as confused as she was.

No tutor can be completely prepared for situations like this, but we can begin to imagine how intense feelings can impact a tutorial session and how we might respond most effectively.

What to Do

When a tutor is faced with a situation involving a traumatic experience the writer had, it is tempting to want to make the writer feel better by responding sympathetically—patting him on the shoulder, sharing a personal experience, or allowing the session to become therapy instead of tutoring. It can be awkward to analyze someone's paper in a professional manner when raw emotions, perhaps some that hit us close to home, inspired its creation. Writers may become defensive or emotional toward our suggestions, unable to step outside the paper and fearful that revising will change its emotional impact.

What is most important in such situations is focus and firmness. We have the complicated responsibility of showing empathy to writers while not allowing them to lose sight of the reason that they came for help in the first place: to express ideas effectively. The problem with emotions, obviously, is that they cloud judgment and rationality on both sides, making for a potentially conflict-filled session. Deep passion for a certain subject or situation can also give otherwise overused topics an entirely new dimension. Imagine a discussion of the adoption process by a woman who surrendered a child when she was eighteen years old, or antiwar sentiments expressed by an ex-marine. When a writer decides to use a personal experience or a deep-seated personal value for an academic paper, it is a tutor's responsibility to help the writer articulate the ideas he has and to provide a fair-minded response, even if it means reaching deep inside ourselves to do so. This point is reinforced in a book by J. A. Kottler, who believes that people who help others can learn a lot about themselves when they have to deal with difficult situations, which may

> force us to be more flexible, creative, and innovative than we ever thought possible. And they require us to look deep inside ourselves to examine every one of our own unresolved issues that get in the way of our being compassionate and effective—both as professionals and as human beings.[3]

Developing a clear goal with the writer for the session is one means of getting some distance from delicate subject matter. This allows the writer not to have to delve into how he feels, and allows the tutor to decide whether she is prepared to give emotional support. While this is an easy suggestion to make, it is difficult and emotionally draining to implement. We are human beings, after all.

In our writing center, we have found the following approaches to be successful in different situations. However, as with all things emotional, each of us has had to experiment to find what is most comfortable and what is appropriate for each new experience.

Acknowledge the difficulty of discussing a personal experience. Whether it is a disclosure of childhood abuse or a commentary on the death of a parent, whether the tutor has had a similar experience or not, it is best to acknowledge rather than ignore the burden of the writer's task. "Congratulations on being able to put this on paper. A lot of people would have a hard time sharing an experience like this," is one way to begin. While this suggestion seems elementary, the writer still needs to hear it. Human beings need to hear that they are being listened to and understood; taking a few minutes to empathize will establish a degree of trust. Now is also the time to remind the writer that tutoring sessions are, in fact, confidential.

Keep pushing the focus that the writer wants to achieve. This is not callous and insensitive when you remember that a tutor is not a therapist; we are limited to offering a tissue, a glass of water, and compassion. Tutors do not have the background or training to offer psychological analysis or counseling. Some would argue that writing itself is the best form of therapy, a theory that tutors probably *do* have the experience to share. (See Chapter 4.)

Imagine, for example, a writer who arrives with a paper in which she is to describe her hero. She has chosen to write about her stepfather, a man who has been a part of her life since she was a very young child. As she wrestles with her gratitude that he is paying for her college experience, on one hand, and her guilt for loving her stepfather more than her birth father, on the other hand, the tutor is spurred to think about her own father and their close relationship. Through the cloudiness of emotions, though, it is clear that the paper is disorganized and lacks a thesis. The tutor's response might be as follows: "You're so lucky to have had him there when you were growing up. Does he know that you're writing this about him?" After allowing the writer to answer, the tutor might then respond, "If you were going to let him read this, what would you want him to get from it?"

With this response, the writer is reassured that her emotions are valid; she is also forced to really think about why she is writing—not simply to tell about the nice things that her stepfather has done for her, but to thank him, perhaps, specifically for being a father when her birth father wasn't there.

If all else fails, suggest that the writer may need some more time. He may need to sort out newly surfaced emotions before trying to present them for a graded assignment. Someone who has recently battled a drug problem or whose best friend was just killed in a car accident should probably not force himself to write about it until the time is right. In this case, a tutor can offer to help in brainstorming another, equally suitable topic. Perhaps the writer will be relieved to learn that it's acceptable to put a piece of writing on a shelf for awhile and that to do so does not show weakness or denial.

Remember that all tutors hope to achieve the same basic goal: to assist others in expressing the ideas they want to convey. Whether the writer's motivation is driven by ego, emotion, or personal growth, the goal should still be the same.

Complicating Matters

Further complicating the issue of sensitivity in tutoring are the tutor's own emotions and opinions and the writer's (intentional or unintentional) use of insensitive or offensive language in papers.

We live in a multicultural society where differences among people are commonplace, though not always respected. Tutors may also have expectations of people that grow out of their own prejudice, such as the mistaken belief that quiet students are unmotivated or that students in basic writing courses are academically weak. Occasionally our prejudices will reveal themselves, and the offended student we are helping may or may not react. This is one of those awkward, inevitable moments in life we all have to learn to deal with. The important thing for any tutor to remember is really quite simple. The moment you realize you have stereotyped or offended the writer, apologize. Then move on, and try never to do it again. Later, do your part to raise consciousness, and for your next staff meeting invite a speaker from your student affairs office to talk about problems of discrimination on campus and how to overcome them (see also Chapter 2).

Inappropriate References for Cultural, Racial, or Ethnic Groups

Sometimes peer tutors are in a unique position to let a writer know, politely but firmly, that he or she has made a racial or ethnic slur. Just about everyone who speaks English knows that there are highly derogatory terms used to refer to African Americans, Native Americans, Asians, Hispanics, Jews, and many other groups. Some, however, are less common: "Gypped" (as in "we had a deal and he gypped me"), for example, is an ethnically derogatory term whose root is the same as that of an itinerant race of people. There are numerous words such as these that are inflammatory and insulting. In addition, tutors need to be prepared to talk to writers about other potentially demeaning references to people, like "Indian" for Native American and "girl" for an adult female. Because many derogatory references are local and regional, you might try exchanging ideas on how to deal with them with other tutors in a tutor notebook.

In some cases, the use of such terms is innocent in that it did not occur to the writer that the term was offensive. Even if the writer is using the term without malice, the tutor needs to make the writer aware of the offending term. Unless the writer intends to provoke a specific response from the audience, the tutor should tell him that some readers will react negatively to what he has written.

Though negative terms stand out and can be easily eliminated, the kind of stereotyping that can be most detrimental tends to lurk beneath the surface; it usually occurs in what the writer appears to be implying about others. This can be harder to talk about because it is easier for the writer to deny and for the tutor to ignore. If the negative implication is fairly clear, however, the tutor should point it out, not ignore it, because the writer needs to be made aware of the reader's response.

Tutors' Emotions

As if tutoring was not complex enough, tutors may also have to deal with their own emotions regarding a particular topic. Because we exhibit the same human vulnerabilities as the writers with whom we work, we are bound to encounter subject matter that we find offensive, hurtful, or heart-wrenching. Specific examples might include helping a writer with a paper about cancer when the tutor has just lost a loved one to the disease, or tutoring a paper about the immorality of homosexuality when the tutor is a homosexual. What should the tutor do when he or she encounters situations such as these?

Before attempting to help another writer, tutors need to evaluate their own feelings about the sensitive topic. Some questions that tutors might want to ask themselves include: Am I able to be objective with this paper? Are my responses going to be emotionally wrought? Can I separate my feelings about this topic from my professional opinion about the merits and faults of the work?

Often the session may go more smoothly if the tutor is simply honest with the writer about his feelings on the topic. The writer can then decide whether or not to continue the session. Consider, for example, a writer who presents a paper in which she colorfully expresses her distaste for the Greek system, and a tutor who happens to be an active member of a fraternity or a sorority. The tutor's response might be, "Now, you say that all the Greeks do is drink beer on the weekends and cause vandalism. Aren't they, historically, philanthropic organizations? Don't most of them, if not all, sponsor charities?" With this response, the tutor is able to reveal his bias while also being devil's advocate as a means to help the writer think about her argument. An opinion paper is nothing, really, if a writer is simply "preaching to the choir," and so part of a tutor's job is to get the writer to consider how this paper might be too simplistic and why she needs to develop a more complete, thoughtful picture. (See Chapter 12.)

There are times when playing devil's advocate can be inappropriate. If a writer comes to the center with a paper that decries homosexuality and the tutor is gay, this is probably not the best time for the tutor to come out. In cases such as this, if another tutor is available, it would probably be better to switch tutors or have two tutors work together to control emotional responses. If no other tutor is available, then tutors must deal with the situation according to their center's policy.

In all cases, if a tutor feels that her personal safety could be threatened as a result of working with a particular writer (as might be the case with a gay tutor assisting a homophobic writer), then the police or campus security should be called. While such cases are rare, it is vital that they be discussed in staff meetings or with the director.

In conclusion, for a writer to make the decision to pour his emotions onto paper and open those emotions up for a classroom grade shows a tremendous amount of strength. Oftentimes writers will come to the writing center for validation that their topic is important and appropriate, not necessarily for the purpose of receiving help, but still making our jobs that much more challenging.

Like any profession that involves more than one person expressing ideas and discussing experiences, tutoring writing is complicated by the emotional responses of everyone involved. Thinking and planning in advance about how to handle emotional situations can make all the difference in a tutoring session. Although highly sensitive sessions remain the exception and not the rule, dealing with them is part of the essence of what we do as tutors: creating an open, respectful, and productive environment for learning to write.

Further Reading

Daniell, Beth. 1994. "Composing (as) Power." *College Composition and Communication* 45 (2) (May): 238–46.

Colleges and university professors, and some tutors as well, are not always receptive to students who write about their religious faith. In this article, Daniell argues that it is a mistake to ignore the connection between religion and empowerment, and she observes that spiritual and religious motives throughout history have actually motivated people to seek literacy. It is troubling, she says, when academics dismiss the spiritual and religious aspects of students' lives. Tutors who are interested in nontraditional students and feminist issues may be especially interested in the interviews Daniell conducted with six women about how they use literacy in their spiritual lives.

Hayward, Nancy. 2004. "Insights into Cultural Divides." In *ESL Writers: A Guide for Writing Center Tutors,* eds. Shanti Bruce and Ben Rafoth, 1–15. Portsmouth, NH: Boynton/Cook.

A tutoring session is never limited to the student's text. It extends into the cultures of the tutor, the writer, and the institution, often revealing new values and perspectives. Hayward's ideas help tutors to see the emotional dimension that often arises when the client and writer come from different cultural backgrounds.

Maxwell, Martha, ed. 1994. *When Tutor Meets Student*. 2d ed. Ann Arbor: University of Michigan Press.

This is a collection of fifty-four diverse and interesting stories written by tutors at the University of California–Berkeley. Their accounts depict life experiences in the writing center on such topics as gender relationships, cultural diversity, plagiarism, and tutor dependency. These stories are told in the tutors' own words and make for great reading.

Payne, Michelle. 2000. *Bodily Discourses: When Students Write About Physical Abuse, Sexual Abuse, and Eating Disorders*. Portsmouth, NH: Boynton/Cook.

This book explores ways in which writing teachers can be most helpful to students writing about these sensitive topics.

Notes

1. This point is developed nicely by Steve Sherwood in "Ethics and Improvisation," *Writing Lab Newsletter* 22 (4) (1997): 2.
2. National Conference on Peer Tutoring in Writing, The State University of New York at Plattsburgh, Nov. 6–8, 1998.
3. J. A. Kottler, *Compassionate Therapy: Working with Difficult Clients* (San Francisco, CA: Jossey-Bass, 1992), xi.

Works Cited

Kottler, J. A. 1992. *Compassionate Therapy: Working with Difficult Clients*. San Francisco, CA: Jossey-Bass.

Sherwood, S. 1997. "Ethics and Improvisation." *Writing Lab Newsletter* 22 (4): 1–5.

6

Crossing Cultures with International ESL Writers

The Tutor as Contact Zone Contact Person

Carol Severino

Most assignments that students bring to the writing center concern subject matters that are inextricably embedded in the contexts of U.S. culture and history. For example, students in our writing center frequently request help with assignments about education, which is one of the most popular themes in the textbook *Conversations*, the most popular composition reader in our first-year Rhetoric program.[1] These writing assignments automatically assume students' familiarity with the U.S. educational system based on a presumed twelve plus years of attending U.S. schools. A glance at the readings about the other controversies in *Conversations* (Language, Race and Gender, Family Matters, Civil Liberties, and Science and Society) reveals that the first four themes might as well have the phrase "in the United States" appended to each. In the case of the fifth theme, Science and Society, *Society* means American society. Composition, and higher education in general, has experienced reforms in the area of diversity, but such diversity is national, not international. When composition anthologies are advertised and marketed as *multicultural*, it means that the texts feature readings by and about U.S. minorities (African Americans, Latinos, Native Americans, Asian Americans). In other words, the "many cultures" of the essays' authors and topics are hyphenated American ones, but not cultures of other nations such as Mexico, Japan, or France. In multicultural readers, we find essays by and about African Americans, but not Africans; we find essays by and about Latinos, but not Latin Americans. International or cross-cultural readers do exist, for example, *One World, Many Cultures*,[2] as do internationalized composition courses, but as Matsuda and Silva point out, they are rare compared to American cultural studies–based anthologies and courses.[3]

41

Some Background

Using U.S.–specific themes in composition courses is understandable, even desirable, because a principal goal of many first-year writing courses is to encourage American students to critically reflect on what they have learned about American history in American schools and to examine and evaluate their experience of American culture. Likewise, in many colleges, the majority of the students taking composition have attended American elementary and high schools. However, a U.S.–based curriculum often not only baffles, but disempowers international ESL students, forcing them to perform in a field that is not only linguistically uneven, but culturally full of potholes. The cultural challenges facing international ESL students also pose challenges for their tutors in the writing center.

What should writing center tutors do when international students must analyze readings about U.S.–based issues and themes? For example, how do they help international students analyze essays on education by Jonathan Kozol, when these students lack first- or even secondhand knowledge of how race and class play out in American neighborhoods and classrooms? How do tutors help international students compare and contrast Malcolm X's and Martin Luther King Jr.'s rhetoric when they do not know their respective roles in the Civil Rights Movement nor how their legacies resonate in American culture? How do they help international students evaluate the appeals of an essay about the role of the 1969 Stonewall riot in the U.S. gay rights movement when the movement itself may even be more foreign to them than the English language in which it is discussed? Composition courses are not content-based as are courses in history or sociology, which evaluate the students' knowledge of movements and key figures; instead, they are courses that focus on thinking, writing, and rhetorical abilities. However, composition courses undeniably possess a hidden curriculum that assumes knowledge of or at least familiarity with U.S.–based cultural content. If communication and content are interdependent, and communication is about unfamiliar content in an unfamiliar language, how can that communication not suffer? In some cases, composition instructors directly "teach the controversy" under discussion by explaining historical and cultural background information, but in other cases, they merely give students a choice of essays in the anthology that have not been discussed and ask them to use a rhetorical method taught in class to analyze one or more of them. Sometimes international students do not even understand why a phenomenon is considered a controversy. For example, a University of Iowa tutor recently had to explain to his international student why the phrase "under God" in the Pledge of Allegiance was controversial, that is, after he struggled to explain what the Pledge of Allegiance was in the first place.

Unless they are global in focus, content courses across the curriculum are often as ethnocentric as composition courses. How does a married Vietnamese engineering major critique the college bar pick-up scene for his human sexuality course if he arrived in the United States from Vietnam only a few years ago and has never even been inside a college bar? How does a Hindu student from India find and interpret the Christ symbols in a novel if she is unfamiliar with Christianity? In a humanities course, the professor recently suggested that the students' "way in" to an assignment to define the relationship between nature and community was to discuss their experiences with camping. For many students from outside the United States, however, sleeping in a tent and cooking outdoors are what their nations' poor do in order to survive; these are not activities for leisure and recreation. Camping may have been "the American way" into that assignment, but it did not help my writing center student Lin, the only international student in the course. My experiences with Lin, a first-year business major from China and the daughter of a real estate developer and a journalist, will serve as my case study in this chapter. I tutored her during the summer when she was taking a course called Technology and (U.S.) Society and am tutoring her again now, helping her with papers and speeches for her rhetoric course and papers for her humanities course.

The writing center is often discussed in terms of Mary Louise Pratt's notion of the *contact zone*, a place "where cultures meet, clash, and grapple with each other."[4] Just as tutors mediate between American students and the seemingly foreign cultures of specific methods like literary criticism or rhetorical analysis, or of specific content like Buddhism, Islam, the Russian novel, or African folktales, they must also mediate between international students and their particularly American or Western assignments. Writing center tutors, then, act as cultural mediators or Contact Persons in the Contact Zone.[5]

What to Do

Crossing Cultures: Tutoring Reading

To help international students address writing assignments about U.S. culturally based readings, tutors must often become reading tutors before or while they are writing tutors. A student must know how to read and understand an essay and know how it fits into the conversation or debate in order to analyze it and write about it. If a target reading is short, tutors and students can take turns reading key paragraphs aloud, with opportunities after every paragraph for students to ask questions about purpose, audience, and historical and cultural references. Or, the tutor can predict which references might cause difficulty and ask students if they understand them. In the Kozol article,[6] Lin said she was not sure about the relationship between property taxes and local funding for schools because Chinese schools are funded by the local governments. In the Stonewall article, she didn't know what the words *transvestites* or *hustlers* meant.[7] Tutors and students can work together to read rhetorically and find claims and support in the first few pages of a reading. Then students can outline the rest of the essay at home, formulating questions about places in the text that are confusing. Another strategy, recommended by educator John Bean, is for teachers and tutors to create reading guides that explain unfamiliar cultural codes.[8] Tutors and students could create these guides together—glossaries of important terms and people that students keep in a notebook. In the role that Judith Powers called the *cultural informant*,[9] we tutors do not necessarily have to give students crash courses in American history, especially when certain periods and events may also be fuzzy in our own minds. After all, tutors may not be American history majors, and like their students, they may not have been born during the U.S. Civil Rights Movement or the Stonewall Riots. However, we can fill in the context with what we do know or remember, ask other writing center instructors for background, or look it up together in an encyclopedia or online with Google, EBSCO Host, or Nexus/ Lexus.

By no means, though, should we tutors assume that international students are blank slates about American issues. Because the curriculum in many European and Asian countries is more international as well as more rigorous than it is in the United States, international students may know more about American history and culture than we suspect they do, or even more than some of our native-speaking American students do. Tutors should ask them about, and help them extrapolate from, analogous situations in their own countries. Tutors need to get to know their students so they can find the level or point at which they can relate to the issue at hand. For example, having grown up in a Communist country, Lin has more insights than American students into her humanities course discussion of the Good Society, especially the issue of equal opportunities for work and play for people of all socioeconomic classes; China has experimented with the distribution of work through communal agriculture and industry in ways that the United States never has. Although she had never attended a poor urban high school in the United States, she had attended an elite high school in China, and for a year she was an exchange student in a small-town high school in Iowa. Because the Iowa high school had more extra-curricular activities and academic choices than the Chinese school, but a weaker core curriculum, Lin was already aware of certain disparities in resources between high schools. Our task as tutors is to help international students find their "way in" or connection to the assignment topic by asking them questions about their relevant experiences or by having them write about their interests and perceptions, as Elizabeth Robertson recommends.[10] As Contact Persons in the Contact Zone, our goal is to help find points of contact and intersection between the student and the assignment.

For more open-ended tasks, such as the humanities assignment about the relationship between nature and community, the tutor may have to help the student find a topic from her own culture and experience that she can discuss knowledgeably and comfortably. Lin had never been camping; when she and her family visit a park or natural wonder in China, Lin says, they usually view it from the car. However, when I was helping her research PFC (perfluorocarbon) pollution in the United States, she told me that she studied environmental issues in high school in China. After two brainstorming conversations to find a personal experience with or in nature, Lin decided to base her paper on her high school's participation in a reforestation campaign to prevent dust from erosion from blowing into urban areas and causing respiratory problems. Then she linked the Chinese Daoist philosophy about the dependence of community on nature to the course readings by Wendell Berry and others. Here are the first two paragraphs of her draft about how China was before the environmental awakening that inspired her high school's campaign.

> Being a girl from China, where ideas and values are changing and renewing everyday, plus studying in America give me unique experiences. My life is full of conflictions between modern and traditional China, between West and East.
>
> I remember when I was little. I heard a lot about how people made lots of money by destroying the environment. In that time, China had just started its economic revolution; people would do anything to make money. Hundreds of thousands of trees were cut down and sold for money; lakes were filled by soils to create more agricultural fields; numerous chimneys suddenly appeared and started to release tons of black clouds; cities became dark and countries became treeless. People were making money, but they were also losing their faiths; people didn't talk to others as they used to; doubts were growing everywhere while communities were falling apart. After I grew up, I looked back and felt that the country was like a child tearing up mom's expensive clothes to make new outfits for a barbey.

The most rewarding way to cross cultures is to converse over time with international students about our perceptions of cultural differences and build toward a mutual understanding. University of Iowa tutor Jeffrey Swenson tells the following story about how he and his Korean student discuss their differing experiences with natural space:

> In one of our first meetings he wrote about the amount of "natural space" he found in Iowa City. He commented that he spent the first three days snapping digital photos of the many jackrabbits he saw hopping around campus. I tried to explain to him that rabbits and deer were common in suburban areas, and that these were not what I would call *natural spaces*, a term I reserved for more remote, wild spaces like Northern Minnesota or Alaska. We talked about how far he would have to travel to see some of these "true" nature areas, perhaps to see a moose or bear, and this developed into a discussion of the size of the United States, as well as the ability to move freely between it and Canada. He talked about the wild areas in North Korea and the near impossibility of visiting there, at least at present, which led into a discussion of the side of his family that he has never met, as they live in North Korea, and have been unable to communicate with relatives on his side of the border since before he was born.
>
> The size and relative wealth of the United States allow me to experience space in an entirely different way than my student, whose life in Seoul seems to be more focused on cultural and familial experiences in the city. My student

was continually amazed by the way Americans waste space, and I was continually interested in the way he lived within what seemed to me to be such tight boundaries, but boundaries that seemed natural to him.

Crossing Rhetorics: Discussing Discourses and Styles

Acting as a rhetorical informant is part of the role of cultural informant, as international students may not be as familiar as American students with U.S. academic genres and conventions. Some of our coaching may sound the same as it does when we tutor native speakers: for example, making sure students use quotation marks and cite the source when they are using someone else's exact words, using scholars' last rather than first names, making sure they know the difference between summarizing or describing versus analyzing, evaluating, or arguing. University of Iowa tutor Galen Reddin finds that many international graduate students he has worked with see academic work as more descriptive than argumentative. They do not realize that they have to defend and justify their choice of focus in a dissertation proposal. For example, a nursing student from Korea simply described the current situation of hospital dismissal and home care for elderly female cardiac patients and provided mortality rate statistics, believing that her description and the statistics would speak for themselves. To her, the need for her research focus was self-evident and did not need to be defended; through her study, she reasoned, the elderly female cardiac population would obviously be helped by living longer. Galen suggested that her discourse was still too descriptive and neutral and that even though it seemed she did not want to sound confrontational on the page, she needed to argue the case that her research focus was necessary and important and would contribute to the field of nursing as well as help this population.

Likewise, smaller stylistic features that we find in international students' papers may be different than what we find in native English–speaking U.S. students' papers. For example, Lin's list of short sentences in her humanities paper are separated by semicolons, a style she says she uses in Chinese. At first I thought she should change the punctuation, because rarely, except in lists, does one find one semicolon after another. Then I realized that sentences punctuated by semicolons rather than by periods and capital letters contribute to Lin's unique poetic, almost hypnotic style. In her rhetorical analysis paper for her rhetoric course, she overquotes from Kozol's essay, but not with long block quotes as native English–speaking American students typically do, but with quoted phrases interspersed among her own words. In the following passage she is contrasting the suburban and urban high schools that Kozol visited.

> As Kozol describes, New Trier has "superior labs and up-to-date technology," and "seven gyms as well as an Olympic pool." At the same time, Du Sable has only "makeshift equipment," a three-story building "in fairly good repair," and a "full-sized playing field and track," in contrasting with the surroundings, which are "almost indescribably despairing."

When I remarked that her numerous interspersed quotations reminded me of the *yijing* form of literary criticism that Fan Shen discussed,[11] Lin said she uses this style of quoting in her papers in Chinese. Her final draft had fewer quoted phrases and received a good grade, but like her humanities paper, it still sounded and looked rhetorically different, the kind of hybrid text that U.S. readers will gradually become more accustomed to in a global society in which English, or rather various World Englishes, are the language of communication.

We often advise our international students to frontload their essays and write deductively rather than inductively when we find their main idea in the last rather than the first paragraph of the paper. They may be writing inductively because of cultural values, using what John Hinds has called reader-responsible rhetoric to be subtle and avoid insulting the reader,[12] but they may also be writing inductively because, as with native English–speaking students, they have only just discovered their main point in the course of writing their draft. Our task as tutors is to discover through dialogue the cause(s) of their inductive presentation of ideas and then discuss why they should change or keep their organizational format.

Crossing Languages: Explaining Word Meanings and Forms

Tutors' roles as Contact Zone Contact Persons and culture-crossers often involve exchanges with students about the meanings, uses, and forms of words, as words and their equivalent or approximate translations have resonances and connotations that vary by culture, language, and experience. To use Pratt's contact zone language, our writing center tutors may encounter many examples of lexical "clashes" with which they and their students "grapple."[13] For example, University of Iowa tutor Ben Otto recently grappled with a matter of register and context with a Japanese student. He explained why, in a paper about drug testing and the invasion of privacy, it is more appropriate to use the term *urinate* rather than *pee* to explain how the test is done. Tutor LuAnn Dvorak was recently confused by a Thai nursing student's draft of interview questions about Iowans' activity levels. The student had written the question, "Are you able to mow the farm?" but told LuAnn that she meant with a push lawnmower, not a tractor. LuAnn, who grew up on a farm, writes,

> Sitting there imagining a farmer pushing a lawnmower over 160 acres puzzled me. Then after sharing questions and explanations about farms in our respective countries, I turned her paper over and drew the layout of a typical Iowa farm, including huge fields, machine sheds, a barn, a garden, and the farmhouse. Around the farmhouse, I drew a yard. That was it. What she meant to ask was, "Are you able to mow the yard?" Not the farm.

Many exchanges about vocabulary involve explanations of humor. Tutor Tracy Slagter's Chinese graduate student who studies humor did not understand why people laughed when Jay Leno told a joke about George Bush being asked about going AWOL in the National Guard. Bush had replied, "No, we have Earthlink." Tracy explained what AWOL meant and how it sounds like AOL, or America Online. The student had heard AWOL many times, but had assumed people were saying "a wall."

The tutor also gives lexical information about word forms. Lin wrote in the first paragraph that I quoted from her Good Society paper that she experiences many "conflictions" between West and East, reasoning well that because *conflict* is the verb form, a different form, *confliction*, would be the noun form, according to what Mina Shaughnessy called "the logic of error."[14] I explained that her reasoning made sense, but that *conflict*, although accented differently depending on whether it is used as a noun or a verb, was both the verb and noun form of the word. Like many international students, Lin needs to be reminded about which nouns are count (like *tree*) and which are noncount (like *soil*). Likewise, *country*, not *countries*, which means *nations*, is the rural counterpart of cities. Unfortunately, when *countries* is changed to *country*, the parallelism between two plural words is lost. I also questioned whether the appearance of Barbie, instead of a doll in general, diminished the seriousness of her discussion of the environment. Then I explained the difference between residential chimneys and industrial smokestacks.

Complicating Matters

Culturally informing in the writing-center-as-contact-zone is a two-way street; it is not something that the tutor does to deposit U.S. cultural information in the student's mind, according to what Paulo Freire called the banking theory of education.[15] Powers makes a clear distinction between the role of tutor as cultural informant and the role of tutor as collaborator,[16] but when both tutor and student are informing one another about each other's cultures, they are collaborators. In our writing center, which has a twice-a-week enrollment program popular among international students, students write informal pieces during their writing center sessions on cultural issues to acquaint their tutors with their lives and their cultures, a kind of contact zone literature that Pratt calls "autoethnographic texts."[17] When I first met Lin and found out that she was from Chang-sha, I lent her Mark Salzman's book *Iron and Silk* to read about how he portrayed her city in the 1980s.[18] In Lin's informal writing composed in the writing center, she updated Salzman's account of Chang-sha as crowded and dirty so that I would not have a petrified, inaccurate image of her hometown. Twenty years later, Lin's Chang-sha is a modern, well-designed city, full of parks and shopping malls.

> Changsha, after thousands of years, has become a city with its unique style. When driving on the street, tall stylist building passing by show you its modernity, while occasionally some stone paths leading to different times remind you of its long history.

I remember a few years ago, the city was busy with changing. There were signs of Under Construction everywhere. When you were walking on the roads, it felt like sands in wind were going to cover every part of you and you would never get out of it. Now, green plants, squares, and parks in the city make almost everywhere a comfortable place to walk and rest, especially along the river going through the city, the Xiang River. There are specially designed pavilions and statues that are perfect for the view. I loved to go there to see the sunsets. The river is colored by the sun's redness, and everything around looks like it's covered in some sort of golden silk. Sometimes there are fishing boats on the river, adding more life color to the picture.

Similarly, it is important for international students to have opportunities to respond to the features of American culture that surround them, both positive and negative, as well as to respond to American perceptions of their own cultures in order to establish reciprocity and a cross-cultural balance. This way, the cultural informing that happens in the writing center is not all American intake with little international output. Here Lin comments positively on American teenagers as compared to Chinese teenagers:

I was an average girl in China with no special skills at anything. All I had was good grade. I didn't think there was anything wrong about that until I cam to America. Everybody around me is so talented. They run, they play music, they play balls, they sing, they do so many activities at school. Besides all that, they work. I had never thought that I should pay my clothes, my car all by myself, but American kids already do. I think this is the biggest difference between American culture and Chinese culture. In China, parents only want their kids to do the best in schools and get the highest score . . . If you go and ask a parent, "Does your kid have to do anything at home?" the answer is probably no. Nobody cares if you can do house work or if you can feed yourself as long as you are a student and have a good grade in school. It's almost opposite here in America. From what I have seen and heard, I think for American parents, the most important thing is that kids know what they are doing and understand it. They want their kids to be able to face problems in their lives. They want them to be able to live by themselves in case anything happens. So American kids may not have good grades as we do, but they know a lot more about real life.

Yet, according to Lin, American teenagers' endless fun activities have a negative downside, and ultimately she prefers her fun Chinese style—in smaller doses she appreciates it more.

American students are having more fun than we are. They have all sorts of dances, Homecoming dance, Valentine's Day dance, and the most important—Prom. Schools organize different kids of activities. I think the most fun ones are the ones during Homecoming week. Unfortunately, those are always expected in Chinese high schools, just never happened, not to my knowledge at least. Actually, we won't have time for those either, since there are too many things we have to learn. I think if an American student went to China, he or she would die there, seriously. He or she would never be able to study from 7 AM to 3 AM the next day or finish tons of hard questions in one night. Another hard thing for the student is that unless he or she is really smart, she would just never have any time to play if she wanted a good grade. We do have poorer social lives in China, but we still find time to have fun, and it turns out to be that the harder you can have fun, the more fun it is.

Because of the year Lin spent in an American high school, her writing has some colloquial characteristics of an immigrant or what Harklau, Losey, and Siegal call a Generation 1.5 student[19] rather than a traditional international student who might not have control over colloquial structures such as Lin's "Nobody cares," "From what I have seen and heard," "go and ask," "does your kid have anything to do at home," "not to my knowledge at least," or "it turns out." In fact, one of Lin's favorite answers to my questions about what she understands of the U.S. cultural content of her assignments, whether true or not, is, "I have no clue." It is tempting to say that the more time a student has studied in the United States, the less cultural, rhetorical, and linguistic informing a tutor does, but with so many subject matters and so much variation in individual backgrounds and experiences, such a formula is too simplistic. We all know of students who have studied in the United States all their lives and are still not sure in what century the Civil War occurred and do not know the difference between the Declaration of Independence and the Constitution.

Crossing cultures in the contact zone, filling in information, closing background gaps, and helping international students find points of contact between their knowledge and experience and their assignments are what make our work as tutors compelling and rewarding. Tutors need to learn from international students about their lives and cultures in order to tutor them better, and international students need to learn from tutors in order to perform better on their assignments. Thus, cultural informing is collaborative when tutors as Contact Zone Contact Persons help their international students find points of contact between themselves and their U.S.–based assignments.

Further Reading

Brice, Jennifer. 1996. "Northern Literacies Northern Realities: The Writing Center in 'the Contact Zone.'" *Writing Lab Newsletter* 20 (5): 1–4. Reprinted in 1998, *The Harcourt Brace Guide to Peer Tutoring*, ed. Toni-Lee Capossela, 168–74. Fort Worth, TX: Harcourt Brace.

Using Pratt's metaphor, Brice describes the writing center at the University of Alaska, Fairbanks, as a contact zone and discusses her interactions as a cultural and rhetorical informant while tutoring a native Alaskan student on revising his personal narrative. She and her student settle on a compromise thesis statement that is in line with the student's cultural preferences.

Severino, Carol. 1994. "Writing Centers as Linguistic Contact Zones and Borderlands." *Writing Lab Newsletter* 19 (4): 1–5. Reprinted in 2002, *Professing in the Contact Zone*, ed. Janice Wolff, 230–39. Urbana, IL: NCTE.

Employing Pratt's framework, Severino demonstrates the many ways in which the contact zone and borderland metaphors fit the writing center site and writing center interactions about culture and language. She discusses "autoethnographic texts" produced in the writing center as contact zone literature.

Bruce, Shanti, and Ben Rafoth, eds. 2004. *ESL Writers: A Guide for Writing Center Tutors*. Portsmouth, NH: Boynton/Cook.

A collection of fifteen chapters on such topics as reading an ESL writer's text, helping writers to clarify their intended meaning, and ESL students' views of the writing center. This book is a valuable resource for any tutor who works with ESL students.

Notes

1. Jack Selzer, *Conversations*, 5th ed. (New York: Longman, 2003).

2. Stuart Hirschberg and Terry Hirschberg, *One World, Many Cultures*, 5th ed. (New York: Longman, 2003).

3. Paul Kei Matsuda and Tony Silva, "Cross-cultural Composition: Mediated Integration of U.S. and International Students." *Composition Studies*, 27 (1) (1999).

4. Mary Louise Pratt, "Arts of the Contact Zone," in ed. Janice Wolff, *Professing in the Contact Zone* (Urbana, IL: NCTE, 2002), 4.

5. Carol Severino, "Dangerous Liaisons: Problems of Representation and Articulation," in *On Second Language Writing*, eds. Tony Silva and Paul Matsuda (Mahwah, NJ: Lawrence Erlbaum, 2001).

6. Jonathan Kozol, "A Tale of Two Schools: How Poor Children Are Lost to the World," in *Conversations*, ed. Jack Selzer (New York: Longman, 2003).

7. Bruce Bawers, "Notes on Stonewall," in *Conversations*, ed. Jack Selzer (New York: Longman, 2003).

8. John Bean, *Engaging Ideas: The Professor's Guide to Integrating Writing, Critical Thinking and Acute Learning in the Classroom* (San Francisco: Jossey-Bass, 1996).

9. Judith Powers, "Rethinking Writing Center Conferencing Strategies for the ESL Writer," *Writing Center Journal* 13 (2) (1993).

10. Elizabeth Robertson, "Moving from Expressive Writing to Academic Discourse," *Writing Center Journal* 9 (1) (1988).

11. Fan Shen, "The Classroom and the Wider Culture: Identity as a Key to Learning English Composition," *College Composition and Communication* 40 (4) (1989).

12. John Hinds, "Reader-Writer Responsibility: A New Typology," in *Writing Across Languages: Analysis of L2 Texts*, eds. Ulla Connor and Robert Kaplan (Reading, MA: Addison Wesley, 1987).

13. Pratt, 4.

14. Mina Shaughnessy, *Errors and Expectations: A Guide for Teachers of Basic Writing* (New York: Oxford, 1977).

15. Paulo Freire, *Pedagogy of the Oppressed* (New York: Seabury, 1970).

16. Powers.

17. Pratt, 5.

18. Mark Salzman, *Iron and Silk* (New York: Vintage, 1986).

19. Linda Harklau, Kay Losey, and Meryl Siegal, *Generation 1.5 Meets College Composition: Issues in the Teaching of Writing to U.S.–Educated Learners of ESL* (Mahwah, NJ: Lawrence Erlbaum, 1999).

Works Cited

Bawers, B. 2003. "Notes on Stonewall." In *Conversations,* ed. J. Selzer, 649–57. New York: Longman.

Bean, J. 1996. *Engaging Ideas: The Professor's Guide to Integrating Writing, Critical Thinking and Active Learning in the Classroom.* San Francisco, CA: Jossey-Bass.

Brice, J. 1996. "Northern Literacies, Northern Realities: The Writing Center in 'the Contact Zone.'" *Writing Lab Newsletter* 20 (5): 1–4. Reprinted in 1998, *The Harcourt Brace Guide to Peer Tutoring,* ed. T.-L. Capossela, 168–74. Fort Worth, TX: Harcourt Brace.

Freire, P. 1970. *Pedagogy of the Oppressed.* New York: Seabury.

Harklau, L., K. Losey, and M. Siegal. 1999. *Generation 1.5 Meets College Composition: Issues in the Teaching of Writing to U.S.–Educated Learners of ESL.* Mahwah, NJ: Lawrence Erlbaum.

Hinds, J. 1987. "Reader-Writer Responsibility: A New Typology." In *Writing Across Languages: Analysis of L2 Texts,* eds. U. Connor and R. Kaplan, 141–52. Reading, MA: Addison Wesley.

Hirschberg, S., and T. Hirschberg. 2003. *One World, Many Cultures.* 5th ed. New York: Longman.

Kozol, J. 2003. "A Tale of Two Schools: How Poor Children Are Lost to the World." In *Conversations,* ed. J. Selzer, 61–63. New York: Longman.

Matsuda, P. K., and T. Silva. 1999. "Cross-cultural Composition: Mediated Integration of U.S. and International Students." *Composition Studies* 27 (1): 15–30.

Powers, J. 1993. "Rethinking Writing Center Conferencing Strategies for the ESL Writer." *Writing Center Journal* 13 (2): 39–47.

Pratt, M. L. 2002. "Arts of the Contact Zone." In *Professing in the Contact Zone,* ed. J. Wolff, 1–18. Urbana, IL: NCTE. Originally appeared in *Profession 91* (1991): 33–40.

Robertson, E. 1988. "Moving from Expressive Writing to Academic Discourse." *Writing Center Journal* 9 (1): 21–28.

Salzman, M. 1986. *Iron and Silk.* New York: Vintage.

Selzer, J. 2003. *Conversations*. 5th ed. New York: Longman.

Severino, C. 2001. "Dangerous Liaisons: Problems of Representation and Articulation." In *On Second Language Writing,* eds. T. Silva and P. Matsuda, 201–09. Mahwah, NJ: Lawrence Erlbaum.

———. 1994. "Writing Centers as Linguistic Contact Zones and Borderlands." *Writing Lab Newsletter* 19 (4): 1–5. Reprinted in 2002, *Professing in the Contact Zone*, ed. J. Wolff, 230–39. Urbana, IL: NCTE.

Shaughnessy, M. 1977. *Errors and Expectations: A Guide for Teachers of Basic Writing*. New York: Oxford.

Shen, F. 1989. "The Classroom and the Wider Culture: Identity as a Key to Learning English Composition." *College Composition and Communication* 40 (4): 459–66.

Wolff, J. 2002. *Professing in the Contact Zone*. Urbana, IL: NCTE.

7

Recent Developments in Assisting ESL Writers

Jennifer J. Ritter[1]

Experienced writing center tutors are accustomed to working with undergraduate, graduate, traditional, and nontraditional students. We quickly learn to change our approaches to accommodate each student's differences. When working with English as a Second Language (ESL) students, we encounter yet another layer of differences. ESL students bring different cultural backgrounds, writing experiences, and English language proficiency to the English writing context. And because many of us are not trained to tutor writers who are working in a second language, our tutoring instincts may short-circuit (see Chapter 6).

As a native English speaker, when I reflect on my tutoring sessions with ESL students, the main difference that I first notice between native speaker and ESL writing is the language. When we read ESL writing, we see expressions or grammatical forms that sound foreign, like a written foreign accent. Unlike native speakers, ESL students may not have high levels of English language proficiency to fall back on. Faced with these aspects of ESL writing, I find it hard to decide whether or not to work on grammatical forms in the tutoring session. Part of my dilemma stems from the fact that I can usually get the gist of the ESL writer's message, and yet, I wonder whether I should still try to help the writer to revise forms and expressions, like verb endings and idioms. I also wonder whether working on these points of language will benefit the students not only with writing, but also with their learning English. As a researcher studying second language acquisition (SLA) and a writing center tutor, I have learned the importance of nonprescriptive negotiated tutoring. But how can negotiation work when there is the added problem of English language proficiency?

Although we are still exploring how we can work best with ESL students, recent research in writing center tutoring and my own field of second language acquisition offers some insights. One insight is that when a tutor and ESL student negotiate meanings and forms in the student's text, the ESL student can improve her proficiency in English. This chapter shares the logic behind this idea of negotiated interaction and how we can use it in ESL tutoring conferences using an experience I had when I worked with a thirty-three-year-old Japanese graduate student named Rika (not her real name).

Some Background

When working with Rika and other ESL students in writing conferences, it seems the dynamics of the tutoring too often change from nondirective to directive approaches. In fact, this change is documented by Judith Powers, who noticed that tutor roles shifted from collaborators to informants when they worked with ESL students.[2] Not only does the tutor role shift more toward informant, but, as Cumming and So acknowledge, there is a stronger tendency to correct errors in the ESL students' texts.[3] From the viewpoint of writing center tutors, these types of conferences contradict our beliefs in nondirective tutoring. As Powers says, we need to devise strategies that are both appropriate for ESL writers and more compatible with writing center philosophy.[4]

In a national survey of writing centers, researchers found that the two most frequent differences in conferences involving ESL writers are the writers' concerns with sentence-level correctness and greater expectations of editing.[5] These differences are to be expected when we consider that unlike native speakers, most ESL students do not have complete fluency in English. When learning a second language, it is rare for anyone to reach a native-speaker proficiency level, or ultimate attainment. This means that most ESL students will acquire grammatical aspects of the language to a certain point and may never go beyond that level. Many ESL students, for example, cannot acquire native-speaker proficiency with grammatical forms such as word choice and word order and will say things such as "Almost it is the same tall as the building." The implication here is that native-speaking tutors may have to include more grammar instruction in ESL tutoring conferences since they have knowledge about English, which their ESL students may need but will probably never attain without instruction.

Errors are a natural aspect of ESL writing, and even though they make the writing sound foreign, not all of them interfere with reading comprehension. As tutors, then, we should learn how to recognize which ESL errors are more serious and can affect reading comprehension. Global errors affect reading comprehension and can include word choice, relative clauses, and word order.[6] An example of a word choice error appears in a paper that Rika wrote about earthquakes when she described how she tried to protect her home. She wrote, "I leave curtains closed because if glass of the window is broken, the curtains *shoot* down from a piece of glasses into the room." In this sentence, a native speaker might interpret "the curtains *shoot* down" in a couple of ways: "the curtains will fall down because of the breaking glass" or "the curtains will keep the broken glass from flying into the room." Since the word *shoot* makes the meaning of this sentence unclear, this error creates a comprehension problem.

Local errors, on the other hand, include things like articles, prepositions, and pronoun agreement, and they usually do not affect reading comprehension.[7] Article and preposition errors are also some of the most difficult for the second language learner to master. These seemingly simple grammatical forms are also among the most difficult for native speakers to explain. Try explaining, for instance, why English uses the preposition *at* for both "I am at school" and "The party is at seven o'clock." If we say that *at* is used for both place and time, then why do we also say, "I am in school" and "The party is on Sunday"? When it comes to local errors like this, there is not much to negotiate and the best thing is simply to tell the writer which words to use.

We can also draw from second language acquisition research to decide how to work with ESL students on language problems. One theory that can be applied to the writing center tutoring context is the interaction hypothesis. One idea behind this hypothesis is that ESL students can learn English through conversation with native speakers.[8] In other words, if the ESL writer's message, whether it be spoken or written, is unclear to the native-speaker tutor, then the two of them can negotiate the meaning of the message. The ESL student, then, is pushed to modify his or her language. Here is an example of negotiated interaction between Rika and me:

Jennifer: So, can you tell me what your paper is about?

Rika: This paper is about earthquakes in Japan. I talk about *evacuating drill* in school.

Jennifer [Initiating negotiation]: I am not sure what you mean. Are you talking about an *evacuation* drill where the students and teacher practice for earthquakes?

Rika [Modifying her language]: Yes, I talk about evacu . . . evacuation, is that right?

Jennifer: Yeah.

Rika: Okay, it is about evacuation drill. Does it make sense to you?

Jennifer: Yes, it does.

As a result of the negotiation, Rika modified her language.

In sum, writing center tutors must recognize that English language proficiency can be problematic in ESL writing. Where the ESL student needs assistance, in this case, is with native-speaker intuitions about English. These intuitions help push the ESL student to recognize his errors. Strategies that we can use to accomplish this can be adapted from second language acquisition research that suggests that conversation and negotiation help in correcting language errors.[9] Negotiation not only allows the tutor to understand the message more clearly, it also provides the speaker an opportunity to develop language proficiency. The implication for the writing center context is that we should negotiate both the meaning and the grammatical forms of the text in order to assist ESL students in improving their writing and grammar.

What to Do

Negotiate the Agenda

We negotiate the agenda with ESL writers as we would with native speakers. We should ask about the student and his writing assignment, beginning with larger rhetorical concerns. The difference, however, is that ESL students will want help with grammatical correctness at some point,[10] and since ESL grammatical errors can affect reading comprehension, these are the errors that should be negotiated during the tutoring session.

Since negotiated interaction, in the sense that it is presented in this chapter, may not seem like a normal conversation, it is helpful for the tutor and ESL writer first to talk about how they will work on language problems. At the beginning of the session when we are learning about the student's needs, we should discuss how best to negotiate. For instance, having the writer read the paper aloud may not work best for him. When a student has a low level of English proficiency, reading aloud may focus attention away from the writing and onto pronunciation, which is not our goal. Rika, for example, felt that she ought to try to read her paper without making any mistakes because errors would be embarrassing for her, even though she knew that the tutor would not mind. But reading aloud may not be an issue with every ESL writer, and we should ask whether they are comfortable reading aloud.

I recommend talking with ESL writers about how to assist them with their grammar. If, for example, you will be reading the paper to the student, you might ask whether she prefers that you pause, repeat, or stress certain words when you notice an error. On the other hand, if the student will be reading the paper aloud, try to devise some other techniques to signal an error. You might raise your hand, point to a word with your pencil eraser, or ask questions. This is how Rika and I negotiated the agenda.

Jennifer: So, Rika, I would like to know if you would like to read your paper to me or if you want me to read your paper to you.

Rika: Can you read it?

Jennifer: Yeah. So, if I am reading it, I need to tell you how I will point out some grammar errors. Listen to me and if you hear me *stress* some words or phrases, or if I just stop reading, I am trying to show you that it doesn't sound right to me. Does this make sense?

Rika: I think so. I will try to listen for this.

Whatever you decide to do, choose techniques you will both be comfortable with. Over time, this type of conversation will seem natural.

Negotiate the Meaning and Form

In ordinary conversation, speakers often negotiate the meaning when misunderstandings arise. With ESL students, these misunderstandings can be a result of language proficiency. As a conversational strategy, negotiating meaning in the writing center conference can help students notice areas that create comprehension problems. For English language proficiency, negotiation of meaning will most likely arise from global errors involving word choice, relative clauses, and word order.

We can negotiate the meaning and form of a text when we want to confirm our understanding or when we do not know what the writer meant. When I was working with Rika, for example, I needed to confirm my understanding of her text where she wrote about another precaution she takes against earthquakes. She said, "I turn off the gas if I am using because of a fire." As a native English speaker, I was not exactly sure what Rika was attempting to say, and I tried to slow things down so that she could discover how to clarify the meaning herself.

Rika [Reading her paper]: I always do when an earthquake strikes. First, I turn off the gas if I am using because of fire.

Jennifer [Initiating negotiation]: Hmm, "if I am using because of fire"?

Rika: Yes, the gas may cause fire.

Jennifer: Oh, so you turn off the gas to *prevent* a fire?

Rika: Is that how to say it? Prevent?

Jennifer: Yeah. If you want to keep something from happening, we use the verb *prevent*.

Rika: How should I write it? First I turn off the gas . . . um . . . prevent fire?

Jennifer: That's close. I turn off the gas *to* prevent a fire.

Rika: Okay. I turn off the gas to prevent fire.

Through negotiating the meaning in this sentence, Rika first realized that she did not know which word to use in this context and then, with help, used the correct form.

If I were reading the paper aloud to Rika, I would try to negotiate the meaning by again slowing things down and emphasizing areas that do not sound right. I might stress certain words or pause at points. If Rika did not realize that I was trying to get her to notice this part of her paper, I would keep repeating the words or phrases and then try to negotiate with her.

Jennifer [Reading paper, initiating negotiation]: My family is prepared to precaution . . . *to precaution* for earthquakes. *To precaution?*

Rika: Is something wrong?

Jennifer: This phrase just does not seem to work. "My family is prepared to precaution." What do you think?

Rika: I don't need precaution?

Jennifer: Yeah, you just need to say my family is prepared.

Rika: My family is prepared for earthquakes?

Jennifer: Yep. It makes sense just to say my family is prepared for earth-quakes.

Again, Rika's problem is language proficiency and she was overgeneralizing the use of the noun *precaution* and used it as a verb. As native-speaking tutors, we can help the writer then notice these areas and negotiate how to revise the problem.

Another consideration whenever we are working with ESL students on grammatical form is whether to focus only on global errors or local errors such as articles and prepositions. In general, articles and prepositions do not cause any serious difficulties with reading comprehension and they should not be a high priority for tutors, according to Harris and Silva.[11] When I quickly read Rika's sentence, "Also I leave curtains closed," I understood the meaning and did not immediately notice that there is a missing article. Although it sounds foreign, the error is not serious enough to spend a lot of time helping Rika figure out what is wrong and how to correct it. I would spend time on this error type only if there were no serious errors in her paper.

Online ESL Tutoring: Provide Models

When we treat grammar and language proficiency problems in ESL writing online, we need to model the language forms for the writer. Although online tutoring does not have the convenience of moment-to-moment negotiated interaction, it is still possible to help ESL writers notice and correct language problems. When I notice global errors in an ESL writer's paper, I first respond with my questions about what I think the writer intended to say. Then, I model corrections as in the following example.

Rika's text: In serious case such as a big earthquake, students had to leave at the school with teachers until someone from home comes to pick them up.

My Comment: Rika, so, are you saying that (1) the students stay at the school with the teachers until someone comes to pick them up? Or, are you saying that (2) the students leave the school and wait with their teachers somewhere else? If you are saying (1), in English we usually say something like "the students had to *stay* at the school with the teachers." If you are saying (2), we usually say something like "the students had to *leave school with their teach-ers*." Does this make sense?

With my questions, I am showing Rika that I misunderstood her message with the intention that she notice a language problem in the sentence. I also wrote two possible corrections to provide Rika with a model of the grammar. The emphasized text is used to direct Rika's attention to what I believe is the specific problem, which is her use of the verb *to leave*. Providing language models is important for ESL online tutoring because the ESL student may not know how to correct the language when the correction deals with forms he may not have attained yet. (See also Chapter 15.)

Complicating Matters

In an ideal world of writing center tutoring, we would be able to follow a few simple steps in each tutoring session that would allow the writer to improve her writing and the tutor to feel a sense of accomplishment. ESL tutoring is no exception. Steps such as negotiating the agenda, meanings, and forms may not always work in a straightforward manner to help the writer improve, however. Here are some problems that you may experience when tutoring ESL students.

You may have the feeling that all the problems in ESL writing stem from language proficiency. This would be an overgeneralization, however, because it does not account for other factors that can affect ESL writing including cultural background and writing abilities. Though it is quite possible that ESL students will need help only with language, as Rika did, this will not always be the case and we should plan to approach each situation with a focus on the student's meaning, discussing matters of grammar as the need arises.

A challenge for any tutor committed to negotiating meaning and form is ensuring that the writer discovers problems on his own. When the ESL student is unaware of language errors due to limited language proficiency, it would be all too easy for us to take a directive role because we have knowledge that the ESL student lacks. The problem, then, is to get the student to notice that the form is incorrect and then to correct it while the tutor remains nondirective. With global errors especially, we want to negotiate because it *slows* the conversation and allows the student more time to process information. In other words, negotiation creates a learning moment. It is not possible to spell out procedures to unfold this process of negotiation. Instead, tutors need to try out different approaches, including the ones described here, and find what works best.

I have presented a way to make the ESL student responsible for her writing while also allowing the tutor to take on the role of informant. Further research in ESL tutoring is needed, however, and writing center tutors are in a good position to conduct this research. For instance, we need to examine how we can address cultural attitudes toward writing that may conflict with American academic writing conventions. (An interesting and useful book on this topic by Helen Fox is in the further reading section.) We also need to explore how we can work most effectively with ESL students during the short time period that we have to work with them. By studying any of these questions, among others, tutors can help to ensure a better fit between ESL tutoring and the nondirective approach of writing centers.

Further Reading

Bruce, Shanti, and Ben Rafoth, eds. 2004. *ESL Writers: A Guide for Writing Center Tutors*. Portsmouth, NH: Boynton/Cook.

This is one of the few books devoted to working with ESL writers in the context of a campus writing center. It is divided into three parts: *Cultural Contexts* looks at the many challenges students face as they learn English. *The ESL Tutoring Session* is packed with new perspectives and helpful tips. And *A Broader View* offers insights into the conventions of English and the stories of ESL students who visit the writing center.

Fox, Helen. 1994. *Listening to the World: Cultural Issues in Academic Writing*. Urbana, IL: NCTE.

The author discusses the difficulties that students from other cultures face in American universities, explaining how cultural values such as indirectness and collectivity make it hard for ESL students to learn U.S. academic writing. This book is useful for any tutor who wishes to learn more about how culture can affect both writing and conferencing. The last chapter, "Helping World Majority Students Make Sense of University Exceptions," is especially helpful for working with cultural issues in tutoring conferences.

Harris, Muriel, and Tony Silva. 1993. "Tutoring ESL Students: Issues and Options." *College Composition and Communication* 44: 525–37.

This article is highly recommended for any tutor or writing center director who wants to learn more about tutoring ESL students. Harris and Silva explain some of the issues related to ESL writing including error types, cultural preferences in writing, and writing process differences. Harris and Silva also provide tutoring suggestions for these issues.

Severino, Carol. 1993. "The 'Doodles' in Context: Qualifying Claims About Contrastive Rhetoric." *Writing Center Journal* 14: 44–61.

Contrastive rhetoric is a term in the field of second language acquisition used to describe cultural orientations that writers have toward texts. Severino explains the controversies related to contrastive rhetoric and the implications for ESL tutoring. This article is appropriate for tutors who would like to learn more about contrastive rhetoric and ESL tutoring.

Thonus, Terese. 1993. "Tutors as Teachers: Assisting ESL/EFL Students in the Writing Center." *Writing Center Journal* 13: 13–26.

Thonus discusses three approaches to teaching and tutoring ESL writing: focus on form, focus on the writer, and focus on the reader, providing examples along with an explanation of the teaching approach. This background information in combination with suggestions for tutoring make this article beneficial for any tutor working with ESL students.

Notes

1. I would like to thank Akiko Suzuka and Yasuko Ono for the useful discussion on ESL tutoring and for providing the ESL writing examples.

2. Judith Powers, "Rethinking Writing Center Conferencing Strategies for the ESL Writer," *Writing Center Journal* 13 (1993): 40.

3. A. Cumming and S. So, "Tutoring Second Language Text Revision: Does the Approach to Instruction or the Language of Communication Make a Difference?" *Journal of Second Language Writing* 5 (1996).

4. Powers, 40.

5. Judith Powers and Jane Nelson. "L2 Writers and the Writing Center: A National Survey of Writing Center Conferencing at Graduate Institutions." *Journal of Second Language Writing* 4 (1995): 125.

6. Joy Reid, *Grammar in the Composition Classroom* (Boston: Heinle, 1998), 126; Robert J. Vann, Daisy E. Meyer, and Frederick O. Lorenz, "Error Gravity: A Study of Faculty Opinion of ESL Errors," *TESOL Quarterly* 18 (1984): 432.

7. Reid, 126; Vann et al., 432.

8. Susan Gass, Alison Mackey, and Teresa Pica, "The Role of Input and Interaction in Second Language Acquisition: Introduction to the Special Issue," *The Modern Language Journal* 82 (1998): 302.

9. Gass et al., 302.

10. Muriel Harris and Tony Silva, "Tutoring ESL Students: Issues and Options," *College Composition and Communication* 44 (1993): 533.

11. Harris and Silva.

Works Cited

Cumming, A., and S. So. 1996. "Tutoring Second Language Text Revision: Does the Approach to Instruction or the Language of Communication Make a Difference?" *Journal of Second Language Writing* 5: 197–226.

Gass, S., A. Mackey, and T. Pica. 1998. "The Role of Input and Interaction in Second Language Acquisition: Introduction to the Special Issue." *The Modern Language Journal* 82: 299–305.

Harris, M., and T. Silva. 1993. "Tutoring ESL Students: Issues and Options." *College Composition and Communication* 44: 525–37.

Powers, J. 1993. "Rethinking Writing Center Conferencing Strategies for the ESL Writer." *Writing Center Journal* 13: 39–47.

Powers, J., and J. Nelson. 1995. "L2 Writers and the Writing Center: A National Survey of Writing Center Conferencing at Graduate Institutions." *Journal of Second Language Writing* 4: 113–31.

Reid, J. 1998. *Grammar in the Composition Classroom.* Boston: Heinle.

Vann, R. J., D. E. Meyer, and F. O. Lorenz. 1984. "Error Gravity: A Study of Faculty Opinion of ESL Errors." *TESOL Quarterly* 18: 427–40.

8

Shifting Gears

Business and Technical Writing

Carol Briam

After setting out on a summer bicycle trip in the Rocky Mountains, our group of twelve did not take long to break up into two camps—the "tourers" and the "racers." We tourers would take our time cycling to our new destination every day. Sometimes we would take unpaved roads off the main route or sit down awhile to dip our feet into an inviting stream. The racers, on the other hand, would speed off to the day's destination, arriving there before noon.

Different motivating factors were obviously at work. While tourers enjoyed a leisurely pace and the opportunity for friendly banter, the racers were motivated by a personal challenge or perhaps simply the desire to savor a good meal at mid-day and thus avoid the tourers' lunch fare of peanut butter sandwiches by the roadside! Neither group was better. Our cycling style differed . . . but we were all cyclists.

And so it is with business and technical writing. It is no better and no worse than other types of writing, but its style differs from other types of writing that tutors and students may have been taught. Readers of business and technical material are motivated by the need to get a job done—they are not lolling on a beach reading a novel. In fact, readers of work-related documents have some points in common with the Lance Armstrong wannabes in my cycling group.

1. *They like good signposts.* Cyclists in a hurry do not like to pause to figure out which way to go, or risk taking the wrong road. As they whiz by a sign, they want it to tell them clearly what lies ahead. Similarly, busy managers reading a report, or consumers following an instruction manual, depend on an informative title and visual cues such as headings to help them readily understand a document (see Chapter 11).

2. *They like smooth and straight roads.* Smooth, straight roads help racers get to their destination quickly. Racers have no patience for tourers' time-consuming diversions off the beaten path. In the same way, readers of business and technical material want written material that gets to the point in a clear and concise way.

3. *They are human.* Sure, racers may look outer-worldly with their aerodynamic helmets and hunched-over riding positions. But they *are* human and yes, they too love fresh mountain air and great scenery. Readers of business and technical documents are also human. They don't want to read documents that sound as if they were written by, and for, a machine.

In the What to Do section, we look at ways tutors can help students with business and technical writing projects to make sure that their writing has useful headings and visual cues, is clear and concise, and is human. But first let's get some common understanding of what constitutes business and technical writing.

Some Background

In today's world of work, poor business and technical writing takes an incalculable toll in the form of lost time and money, misunderstood instructions, or misguided decision making. Recognizing the importance of business and technical writing, many universities offer courses in these areas. However, distinguishing between the two types of writing can sometimes be a problem. Technical writing—which is traditionally associated with science, engineering, and technology—generally has these characteristics:

1. It should be clear and concise.
2. It depends heavily on numbers due to the often quantitative subject matter.
3. It relies on graphics, such as photographs, tables, and charts.[1]

Yet all of these traits are true of business writing, too.

Because it is difficult to make a neat distinction between business and technical writing, the two types are increasingly referred to jointly as *professional writing* (or *communication*) to include all writing and communication in the workplace.[2] In this chapter, *business writing* and *technical writing* are viewed as merely different shades of the same color, with the term *business and technical writing* used interchangeably with *workplace writing*.

Among the many things that business writing and technical writing have in common, one of them, unfortunately, is a bad reputation. We are exposed to technical writing every day, whether it be in product inserts for medicine or instruction manuals for electronic equipment—and everyone seems to have their own horror story about an especially cryptic set of instructions. As for business writing, it is notorious for being jargon-laden, sometimes to the point of being meaningless. In a parody of this trait, one website offers millions of combinations of business phrases available for writers. With the click of a mouse, writers can randomly "spin" the phrases together to form sentences "ready for inclusion into your business memos without all of the thinking!"[3] Nonsense sentences such as this one get shuffled together: "Recognizing improvement opportunities/sustainable competitive advantage/leads the way with/an enterprise-wide value framework."[4]

By offering courses in business and technical writing, universities are "recognizing improvement opportunities" for this type of writing. Typical assignments in such courses include correspondence and memos, reports, instructions, and presentations. Through these assignments, instructors try to anticipate the needs and requirements of future potential employers. Thus, in writing center consultations related to these assignments, tutors and writers must consider not only the teacher's requirements, but also the imagined requirements of potential employers, who make up a "powerful secondary audience . . . [that] is nearly always casting a rhetorical shadow."[5]

What to Do

Tutors may find that students in business and technical writing courses are initially confused by writing requirements for their courses that differ from, or even contradict, writing guidance they may have received for academic-type research papers or personal essays. The first thing a tutor may need to do is to help the writer understand that *contrasting assumptions* underlie writing done in a work setting and writing done in a school setting. Two important assumptions in university writing are:

1. *The reader (the teacher) is a captive audience.* With university writing, we do not question the fact that the professor will read the student's paper. But in a work setting, there is no captive audience. The reader—whether it be a boss, a colleague, or a consumer—can, and will, run away from the piece of writing if it is not inviting enough or does not meet a need.

2. *The reader (again, a teacher) is the expert.* In university writing, the teacher is the expert, and students must often prove to the teacher that they know a subject and understand its specialized vocabulary. In English classes, students may feel an additional need to use complex syntax or an expansive writing style. The assumption that the writer must prove knowledge to an expert reader can lead people to write more rather than less, and to use complex terms and sophisticated sentences over common words and shorter sentences. Yet in the workplace, such an approach is the opposite of what is needed. The workplace author of a document is probably seen as the expert on the topic at hand. Rather than showing off knowledge, the writer ideally shares only pertinent information so that readers can readily understand an issue or carry out a task.

Once a tutor helps a writer see that the underlying assumptions between school and workplace writing differ, the tutor can then deal with specific issues. At one writing center devoted to business writing, tutors show students who are already excellent writers how to "take their writing to the next level" through editing.[6] Following this approach, I will edit samples of "good writing" to show tutors how the samples can be transformed into "good workplace writing." By observing differences between the two versions, tutors can see more clearly how workplace writing differs from other types of writing. Understanding these differences will prove helpful when tutors try to guide writers toward effective revision. The writing samples to be edited are taken from Joseph M. Williams' book, *Style: Toward Clarity and Grace.*

Headings and Visual Cues

Because the reader of a workplace document wants to be told up front what the main point is, tutors should look for the equivalent of a conclusion at the beginning, with supporting information then following. This can run directly counter to essay writing that often builds up to a conclusion or saves the best for last. The burden to say what a document is about should not be left entirely to the text. Titles also play a key role in defining the subject and purpose of the text. Williams recommends that titles be straightforward like this one:

Before: "Computer Assisted Instruction: Advantages and Disadvantages"[7]

This title can be made to be more informative. Depending on the main point of the document, the title could say:

After: "Computer-assisted instruction: Disadvantages outweigh the advantages" or "How computer-assisted instruction can help us expand our training program"

Tutors can ask writers to think of a title as a type of newspaper headline. After all, the day after a hotly contested mayoral election, a city newspaper would not use as its headline "Election Results." It would print something like "Jones Wins Election by Slim Margin." In this way, the reader who reads nothing more than the headline, or headline-like title, is still gaining valuable information.

Beyond the title, informative headings should be used throughout the document as well. While wording is important, so is visual distinctiveness. Headings should stand out, like stepping-stones across a creek. Some options include: bold face, a larger type size, a box, or extra white space around the heading. Using typography and layout to reveal the structure in a document will help entice the workplace reader to read the document, and then to make his way through it. For example, just by using shorter paragraphs with spacing between the paragraphs, a writer can break up masses of gray text that otherwise might discourage reading. Tutors may need to remind writers that they do not need a topic sentence and a minimum number of sentences for a paragraph to be a paragraph.

Using bullets can also be a good visual tactic to make information stand out. In the following example, Williams shows off a sentence with model parallelism:

> *Before:* The committee recommends that the curriculum in applied education be completely revised in order to reflect trends in local employment and that the administrative structure of the division be modified to reflect the new curriculum.[8]

With slight rewording, we can use bullets to make the important information in this sentence stand out more:

> *After:* The committee recommends these actions:
>
> • Completely revise the curriculum in applied education—to reflect trends in local employment, and
> • Modify the division's administrative structure—to reflect the recommended new curriculum.

An added advantage to point out here is that strong action verbs—usually a plus in workplace writing—replace the passive constructions of "be revised" and "be modified."

While bullets are visually appealing to the reader in a hurry, they are not always the best option for making information clearer. For example, Williams uses bullets to present this information:

> *Before:* . . . [We] must understand three things about complex writing:
>
> • it may precisely reflect complex ideas,
> • it may gratuitously complicate complex ideas,
> • it may gratuitously complicate simple ideas.[9]

The problem here is that the reader is forced to sift through each bulleted item to discover how each one differs from the others. A better option would be to forget the bullets and use a sentence:

> *After:* While complex writing may precisely reflect complex ideas, it may gratuitously complicate ideas, whether those ideas are simple or complex.

Clear and Concise Writing

Most students know instinctively that clarity and conciseness often go together. Reducing unnecessary words usually helps the meaning of a sentence stand out, just as weeding a garden helps the flowers to stand out. The two sentences that follow demonstrate how tutors can show writers how to weed out unneeded words and make the meaning clearer. In these examples, I italicize words that can be eliminated or replaced with fewer words.

Before: We *set for ourselves* two more objectives because *seeming* clarity in professional writing *is a matter that* depends on more than *merely* a writer's *level of* skill.[10]

After: We have two more objectives because clarity in professional writing depends on more than a writer's skill.

Before: Those *who experience* problems with *their* writing *have to understand that they* must approach different causes of bad writing in different ways.[11]

After: Those with writing problems must approach different causes of bad writing in different ways.

In each of these examples, the number of words was reduced by more than one-third, and in the process the main point of the sentence was made to stand out better. Tutors can remind writers that such conciseness and clarity can be a godsend for workplace readers who typically are inundated each day with bulging inboxes, both paper and electronic.

Even when tutors don't understand a text, they can still offer editing advice. Consider the following sentence (take a deep breath first!).

Before: When pAD4083 in the *E. coli pmiimanA* mutant CD1 heterologously overexpressed the *P. aeruginosa pmi* gene, there appeared high levels of PMI and GMP activities that were detectable only when pAD4083 was present.[12]

Williams says that this sentence "is clear to someone who knows the field."[13] Even if this is the case, perhaps we can make the sentence clearer for the specialist who reads it. As a tutor, you may ask, what can I notice about this sentence even if I don't know what on earth it's about?

First, note that the action of the sentence—the passive expression "there appeared"—does not occur until more than halfway into the sentence, after we've already slogged our way through a lot of complex terms. Second, note that something significant appears to be reported at the very end of the sentence, but the reader might overlook it because it is last in line behind a string of weighty words. Wouldn't it be better to bring to the forefront this significant information by means of a separate sentence?

Using this logic, I might edit the sentence this way:

After: High levels of PMI and GMP activities appeared when pAD4083, in the *E. coli pmiimanA* mutant CD1, heterologously overexpressed the *P. aeruginosa pmi* gene. These high levels were detectable only when pAD4083 was present.

Now, I still don't fully understand what this is saying. But I think tutors will agree that the edited version conveys its meaning in a clearer way for those who do understand the terminology. One caveat here: It's always a good idea when editing material that uses unfamiliar terminology to double-check with the author to make sure that errors are not inadvertently introduced in the editing process.

A tutor who demonstrates options for editing writing is motivated not by a need to nit-pick, but by a desire to show writers concrete ways to attain a whittled down, to-the-point writing style. Such an approach, which emphasizes product as much as process, can help satisfy a craving by writers for specific information about workplace genres that may be totally new to them. Martha Thomas, director of a writing center devoted to business communication, recommends that tutors share explicit knowledge about business forms and conventions, thus possibly avoiding an "unnecessarily protracted attempt to prod struggling students into discovering the knowledge for themselves."[14] Sometimes, says Thomas, the "most pedagogically effective thing the tutor can do may be to turn on the headlights and stop relying too heavily on the rearview mirror."[15]

Writing That Is Human

Some tutors might conclude that business and technical writing should be all business and devoid of any personality. Don't let yourself or the writers you work with fall into the trap of thinking this. As William Zinsser says, "just because people work for an institution they don't have to write like one."[16]

One reason workplace writing is often not human is that writers may want to appear smart in front of their boss and colleagues, and so they use pretentious terms. Another potential problem is that workplace writers often use models or templates for their writing. Now there's nothing wrong with this. It's like the guy who, distrusting his fashion sense, observes the mannequins in the men's department to help him figure out what shirts and sweaters go together. A problem would arise, however, if the fashion-challenged guy stopped acting like a human being and assumed a stiff pose with a glazed-eye look. Unfortunately, many workplace writers—relying on model formats—do the equivalent of acting like a mannequin when it comes to their writing. The result can be writing that sounds as if it was written by a robot.

Business writing consultants say that getting workplace writers to write in a more human way can be a big hurdle to overcome. For example, one consultant worked with employees of an insurance company who wrote letters in response to insurance claims. In cases where claims officers responded to widows or widowers requesting survivor benefits, sometimes the only hint of kindness in the letter was the statement: *Please find enclosed a self-addressed envelope for your convenience*. To help these writers craft more human letters, the consultant suggested that they write as if the recipient were a loved one, such as a father or grandmother. This helped the writers to consider thoughtful options, like acknowledging the person's loss before discussing the insurance claim.

The next hurdle for the consultant, however, lay in convincing the supervisors of the claims officers to approve the more human writing. Some bosses believe that incorporating a personalized remark is being unbusinesslike. They don't see that treating the reader like a person, instead of a policy number, can be good for business.

Complicating Matters

When reading a writer's work, tutors may feel as if they're looking through a window smeared with petroleum jelly—everything seems a bit fuzzy. Either the paper refers to subject matter the tutor is not familiar with (such as accounting terminology), or the writing may be full of jargon or abstract concepts. Rule number one is: *Don't be afraid to ask questions.* So many times I've asked managers about something in their writing: "What does this mean?" or "Can you give me an example of this?" And so many times I've seen that either they don't truly understand it or have an unclear notion about it. When questioned, they are forced to explain it in more detail or give examples (and, in some cases, they must seek answers from their organizations). This probing for clarification can be valuable because it can bring up helpful information that supplements or even replaces the original information.

If you don't feel comfortable or your ego risks taking a bruising for asking what is perceived to be a dumb question, not to worry. Try these tactics:

- *Ask the writer to explain something as if he were explaining it to a bright twelve-year-old.* This gets the burden off your shoulders, but still forces the person to reformulate something that otherwise seems too obscure.
- *Have the writer think about whether there are secondary audiences that haven't been considered.* Secondary audiences are often ignored and provide good reason for taking such moves as spelling out acronyms on first reference or providing additional explanations, anecdotes, or examples.

A big complicating matter may be that you don't have any complicating matters. That is, perhaps your writing center doesn't receive any writers with business and technical writing projects. Several reasons could explain this. First, your university may be fortunate enough to have a business writing center affiliated with a school of business. If so, great. You might want to check it out. You can learn something from them, and they can undoubtedly learn something from you and your writing center experience.

But if there is no such specialized writing center at your university, perhaps students in business and technical writing courses don't know that you exist, or they think you cannot help them or are not interested in their type of writing assignments. One good strategy to try to change the situation could be to plan a résumé writing and editing workshop at your writing center. Résumés or CVs (*curricula vitae*) are great documents to work with because

- Writers have a personal stake in making them good.
- They're concise (or they should be).

- They represent a microcosm of workplace writing issues discussed in this chapter. Résumés rely on good visual headings and on clear language with strong verbs. Ideally, they should be personalized somewhat, too.

Most people have trouble writing an effective résumé for themselves because they're too familiar with the jobs and experience they've had. They give in easily to using preexisting job titles and descriptions that may not have much meaning to an outsider. Just talking over the content and presentation with someone in the writing center can yield huge benefits. Besides, it's a good way to introduce your writing center to business, engineering, and other professional majors. (Be sure to put notices about the workshop in areas they're likely to see.)

Naturally, by reaching out to students of business and technical writing, tutors can help these writers. But just as important, tutors can help themselves. By initiating more contact with these writers, you (and your writing center) will develop expertise in workplace writing—expertise that you'll inevitably draw on at some point in your future profession. While you'll be making things easier for future readers of your writing, you may also find, as many have, that the style of business and technical writing makes the actual act of writing easier. . . . It can be like having the wind at your back.

Further Reading

Bailey, Edward P. Jr. 1997. *The Plain English Approach to Business Writing*. New York: Oxford University Press.

A college writing teacher, Bailey says that before discovering plain English, he used to teach a formal style designed to impress rather than communicate. In his book, Bailey practices what he now preaches. The book is succinct and user-friendly with many examples that show how to achieve a writing style that is well-suited to the workplace.

Pfeiffer, William S. 2004. *Pocket Guide to Technical Writing*. 3d ed. Upper Saddle River, NJ: Pearson Prentice Hall.

This book is intended as a compact reference for students and on-the-job writers. Pfeiffer advocates an "ABC" structure—first an Abstract of the main points, then the Body of supporting details, and lastly a Conclusion that wraps up and provides information the reader needs to act. The book includes a helpful chapter on "Graphics and Oral Presentations" as well as numerous examples of formats for different documents, such as "positive" and "negative" letters, feasibility studies, lab reports, and résumés.

Zinsser, William. 2001. *On Writing Well: The Classic Guide to Writing Nonfiction*. 25th anniversary ed. New York: HarperResource.

A journalist by profession, Zinsser devotes two chapters to business/technical writing. One chapter is entitled "Science and Technology" and another chapter is entitled "Business Writing: Writing in Your Job." Once you pick up this book, though, you'll be hard-pressed to limit your reading to just these two chapters. Throughout the book,

Zinsser explains how to put into practice his tenets of good nonfiction writing, including two of the most important qualities: humanity and warmth. As books on writing go, they don't get any better than this one.

Notes

1. Philip Rubens, ed., *Science and Technical Writing* (New York: Holt, 1992), xxi–xxii.
2. Kitty Locker, "Will Professional Communication Be the Death of Business Communication?" *Business Communication Quarterly* 66 (3) (2003): 122.
3. Mike Shor, *MBA-Writer* www2.owen.vanderbilt.edu/mike.shor/Humor/ MBAWriter/, accessed 7 September 2004.
4. Shor.
5. Frank Griffin, "The Business of the Business Writing Center," *Business Communication Quarterly* 64 (3) (2001): 77–78.
6. Deborah Valentine, "A Business Writing Center Serves Writing Requirements in a Pre-professional Program," *Business Communication Quarterly* 62 (1) (1999): 102.
7. Joseph M. Williams, *Style: Toward Clarity and Grace* (Chicago: University of Chicago Press, 1990), 110.
8. Williams, 138.
9. Williams, xi.
10. Williams, x.
11. Williams, x.
12. Williams, 18.
13. Williams, 19.
14. Martha Thomas (personal correspondence, 26 September 2004). Thomas is director of the Center for Business Communication at the Moore School of Business, University of South Carolina.
15. Thomas.
16. William Zinsser, *On Writing Well*, 3d ed. (New York: Harper & Row, 1985), 145.

Works Cited

Griffin, F. 2001. "The Business of the Business Writing Center." *Business Communication Quarterly* 64 (3): 70–79.

Locker, K. O. 2003. "Will Professional Communication Be the Death of Business Communication?" *Business Communication Quarterly* 66 (3): 118–32.

Rubens, P., ed. 1992. *Science and Technical Writing: A Manual of Style*. New York: Holt.

Shor, M. 2004. *MBA-Writer*. Accessed 7 September 2004. www2.owen.vanderbilt.edu/ mike.shor/Humor/MBAWriter/.

Valentine, D. 1999. "A Business Writing Center Serves Writing Requirements in a Pre-professional Program." *Business Communication Quarterly* 62 (1): 101–03.

Williams, J. M. 1990. *Style: Toward Clarity and Grace.* Chicago: University of Chicago Press.

Zinsser, W. 1985. *On Writing Well.* 3d ed. New York: Harper & Row.

9

Is There a Creative Writer in the House?

Tutoring to Enhance Creativity and Engagement

Wendy Bishop

Creative writing. Have you ever wondered what *un*creative writing would be and why anyone would aim for the same? Ditto *un*critical thinking. I believe that all engaged writers are both critical and creative. How could they aim not to be? So even as I offer ideas for looking at the tutoring session with creativity in mind, I don't think of my advice here as merely adding a technique, or spicing up the session, or putting icing on the tutorial cake. Instead, this perspective is meant to encourage you to help writers to think-like-a-writer-thinks (and I hope that's the perspective you take too).

Some Background

Peter Elbow believes that we need to like our writing to perform well at it. Donald Murray says that all writing is to some degree autobiographical. Both claims suggest writers need to be engaged with the text, no matter who assigns it, or for what purposes. Too often, the clients we see in writing centers are lacking a connection, a spark, a perspective. Not unreasonable, given the conditions of institutional schooling. Writers who come to work with us may view writing as not theirs, the role of writer as not theirs, and the joys of writing as forever out of their reach. Giving them some insight, providing them with some writers' rules of thumb and practical practices can often be just what it takes to guide them to greater engagement.

Greater engagement usually equals greater investment. And greater investment—even if it doesn't result in immediate, dramatic improvement in the text at hand—generally has long-term effects. Positive engagement prompts the writer you work with to spend more time with a text. And more time with a text—with that one, this one, and the next one—is the only sure road to better writing. Creative writers know that. They are infamous for telling you how long and hard they work at their craft. "The problem of creative writing," says

74

poet Stephen Spender, "is essentially one of concentration, and the supposed eccentricities of poets are usually due to mechanical habits or rituals developed in order to concentrate."[1]

Lack of concentration, poor work habits, counterproductive rituals push writers away from their texts. So does discouragement. Studies of basic writers in the 1970s and 1980s proved how discouraging text work was for writers who were not supported, encouraged, or engaged. Researchers like Lillian Bridwell-Bowles, Sondra Perl, Nancy Sommers, Mike Rose, and others found that the basic writers they observed and talked to were stuck at the local level—worrying over spelling, worrying over the presentation of self, worrying over a crippling number of lower-level writing issues. They never had a chance to engage, soar, create, discover, learn about self and others, family and community, to think through writing.

Not only that, most student writers just don't make or take the time needed to make significant progress with their writing. And, of course, their lives are busy: "Adrianna provides a profile of work habits typical of other students in her class. She takes five classes, works twenty hours each week, and spends six to ten hours per week on homework," says Susan Wyche in a recent study.[2] Interviewing students like Adrianna, Wyche found that they didn't have the space or habits of concentration that Stephen Spender claims are so crucial to creative work, that we know are crucial to getting work done at all:

> Adrianna has difficulty creating and following through on self-made schedules. Her problems are further compounded by being unable to concentrate for extended periods of time; instead, she takes numerous breaks, including watching television. By her own account she begins drafts cold, using only the hour prior to drafting to give the paper serious thought.[3]

It's not surprising, actually, that tutorials alone can spark creativity in our students by providing them a place and sustained opportunity to think through writing—a place and an opportunity they find or make nowhere else in their busy lives. Writers are people who write. Just that.

No positive feedback? No reason to move forward. No bag of tools and tricks? No alternatives. No time? No place? No plan? Then no way to vault out of a corner, leap out of a pit, improvise, riff, discover, and uncover. Writers need flexible rules of thumb, heuristics, and a sense of when to use what, where, when, how, and why. They need writing center tutors to help them find their ways. So let's look at some.

What to Do

Getting Started

Where do writers' ideas come from? From reading in the broadest sense—reading other writers, reading one's own life, reading the world around us. As a student of poetry and later as a teacher of writing, I learned to read other writers backward. Call this a sort of tongue-in-cheek version of the weighty literary giant deconstruction. "What," I'd speculate, "might have prompted this poem about . . . love, death, life? What can I see going on technically at the word, sentence, whole-text level that I could copy (steal?), celebrate by borrowing? What is going on thematically that resonates to my own life?"

Asking such questions, I'd work backward from product to process. Famous examples? *Romeo and Juliet* becomes *West Side Story.* The laconic prose style of Ernest Hemingway is everywhere imitated. But here's the secret: what works as a technique for uncovering, deconstructing, understanding literary genres holds true of the more technical and transactional genres of writing in our lives. We don't reinvent the phone book each time one is assembled, we alphabetize. We respect a moving college application essay when we read it—and we can analyze it rhetorically to see how the writer appealed to us, moved and persuaded us to see her as the best possible candidate for our program. Web 'zine sites become popular because they "work," but we can look at any textual "work" for its constituent parts—what language does it use, what voice, sentence style, organizing strategy, daring effects? And as tutors we need to help writers come to these understandings—to argue and articulate how they read, what they read, and why they read.

To encourage careful reading and imitation (I mean in the best sense—set by the writer, not set as a lesson in writing-as-punishment),

> **Try What-ifs.** What if I recast my opening paragraph in short declarative Hemingway-esque or circular Gertrude Steinian sentences? Will I be able to harvest a passage of declarative or rhythmically circular prose?

To encourage idea generation if your writer (and you) are short of ideas,

> **Try Something-likes.** Which kind of writing that I admire is something like the writing I'm doing? Then, what of those something-like writings—theme or style or both—might I import into this text?

To explore options, to open up new avenues,

> **Try Lots-ofs.** Lots of X writing goes like this. Therefore, I could do some X and then add some Y writing to vary, complicate, and add interest to my X writing.

And finally,

> **Collect start-up exercises.** Here's where creative writing textbooks can offer you specific, stealable advice, tricks, tools, tries. Realize that an invention prompt for a poem can often add spice to an essay. Michael Walters, for instance, suggests: "Write a line of poetry that seems to be an opening line . . . then be prepared to give your line away . . . [after discussion of the lines] the author of the line agrees to give it—no strings attached and forever—to the student whose suggestion, enthusiasm, or

oddball approach most pleases him/her."[4] I think you can see how this can work in a composition classroom. But it can also work in a one-to-one or small group tutorial where first lines are brainstormed together, discussed, and then "auctioned off," that is, chosen to allow the writer a first start or a solid new start.

Realize that most writers mix and match genres. That inventions work in clusters—writing about memory, food, family, often take us to the same early childhood wells of inspiration. Robin Behn and Chase Twichell have put together a useful book for poets in *The Practice of Poetry.* Natalie Goldberg in her two popular books, *Wild Mind* and *Writing Down the Bones,* offers Zen-inspired prompts and advice. (See Further Reading.) Elaine Farris in *Writing from the Inner Self,* edited by E. F. Hughes, begins with the writer and moves outward, including excellent prompts for descriptively emphasizing the five senses. My own book, *Released into Language,* offers two chapters of multigenre prompts, including writing intentionally clichéd works to learn the perils and uses of clichés. A second book, *Elements of Alternate Style,* encourages stylistic experimentations. And an early tutor training book, *Training Tutors for Writing Center Conferences* by Thomas Reigstad and Donald McAndrew, offers a series of tutorial-based prompts—a composing exercise to get even the most topic-free writer into a topic of personal interest, to development techniques like nutshelling (similar to paraphrasing). (See Chapter 11.)

For creative critical responses, there's no finer resource than Peter Elbow and Pat Belanoff's *Sharing and Responding.* One of my favorite of their response techniques asks a reader to describe "What's Almost Said or Implied." What do you think the writer is going to say but doesn't? What ideas seem to hover around the edges? What do you end up wanting to hear more about?[5] I take this exercise one step further by encouraging the writer to name what prompts him to feel this way about his own texts—are there textual, tonal, or syntactic clues? Can this missing-ness be heard in the writer's voice as she reads aloud to you? The why of it all is what your writer needs to learn—to see with you, to see for himself.

From my use of that book and my collaboration with other creative writing teachers like Hans Ostrom and Katharine Haake, I've developed some "continuing on techniques" that I encourage writers and their tutors to try.

Continuing On by Revising Out

Sometimes a writer has an idea. But not enough text. The writer you're working with has a desire to be engaged, but hasn't gotten rolling so isn't really. Engaged, that is. I ask flat out for what I call a "fat draft." Next draft is doubled. One paragraph must become two, two pages four, and so on. No questions asked, no judgments made. At this point, not (necessarily) better but more.

For the writer who already has a mass of text but isn't ready to revise down (where we cut off rather than open possibilities), I ask for a shadow draft and/or postoutlining. For a shadow draft, the writer reads over his text once, then turns the paper over and returns to the computer or the paper and pen, and begins again. What was most important remains salient and reappears, what was not important has fallen aside. The new draft may be the best draft or the best new draft may be a recombination—a word milkshake—taken from the two. Writers know that sometimes many, many more than two drafts make up the real textual volume of a final text, but shadow drafts somehow sound less threatening. More on shadow drafting can be found in a textbook called *Metro,* by Ostrom, Bishop, and Haake.

Postoutlining   No, outlining isn't all bad. Done to force thought and the writer and the text into a preordained mold, it can constrain and constrict. But outlining can also be a creative tool when used at the right time. Ask the writer to read the text paragraph by paragraph. After each paragraph has been shared, together find the center-of-gravity sentence—the central idea or thesis. If not a single solid sentence, then summarize the gist of the passage in one sentence. Write it down. Go on, find the next one in the next paragraph, and the next. Then look at what's there. Not a B for every A or a II for every I. But a rough skeleton of thought in motion. Now, think about reorganization as potential and possibility. What ghostly, missing paragraphs still could be or need to be written? Why?

Consider together what would happen to this text if the writer changed or mixed genres. We know this happens anyway—the effective argumentative paper often begins with a dramatic narrative lead. Sometimes there may be room for a diary entry, a poem, an aphorism, a quote, in a seemingly straight-arrow, down-the-right-hand-margin, traditional paper. What would, how could you and the writer argue for this? (Hint—most down-the-margin student work is a devalued genre we could label schoolwriting.) What do you and this writer need to do to make yourselves and other in-the-world-writers actually want to get involved with this text? Would you really read on if you didn't have to? If not, take a risk and make this text—at least for one draft—a text you would choose to read.

Predict the future   Finally, where else could this piece go? Characterize its form. Use a metaphor—it looks like a pear, it's got the zig-zagging organization of an English garden maze or a computer game. Is that what seems best for the writer, the occasion, the reader? Decide together on how to capitalize on the strengths of this draft. Talk about this. What is done well and could be done more? Writers need space and excess—lots of words, lots of pages, lots of experiments. Without experimentation, and some falling back for recalibration (let's call it this instead of failure), foreword movement can't take place.

Continuing On by Revising In

Okay. Urban sprawl. We know it. Daily, we enter many arenas of textual sprawl. The windy legal brief. The belabored letter to the editor. The paper where everyone offered good advice and the eager writer—your client, perhaps—added, and added, and added, and now has too many leads, too many paths to take or abandon, too much. Still, this is good. Think of the metaphors at hand: pruning, shaping, selecting, highlighting, dramatizing. (Let's consider these, although even as I put down one metaphor two others grow in its place.)

Prune   Think of this as global and/or local removal of deadweight. Globally. Through postoutlining (yes, maybe a second time), a writer can learn to see repeats. Most of my essays begin three or four times and I find this true of the work I help edit, too. Look for the place where you both want to slap down an arrow and say, "This text starts here." Should the writer trim? reshuffle? reorganize? At the local level, pruning suggests some words need to disappear. After doing sentences, do the same for words: change two to one—the right one, the precise one, the effective one. Tune and tauten. Look for clunky first-breath clauses and sentences and enjoy trying them six different ways, together. You each write three. You both vote. One stays. The writer has pruned the original down and tossed other attempts. It's worth it. You find confusing words and play dictionary and thesaurus together—what do you think this word means? What does it generally mean? How is it meaning here, and is it meaning what the writer thinks it means and needs it to mean?

Shaping and selecting   What textual space does the writer really have? Has he written two thousand words in pursuit of a solid five-hundred-word response? That's fine. Shape and select. Does he want something circular? This is good in a long piece where he may need to remind us of the beginning when we reach the ending. But in a small five-hundred-word space, maybe the economical traditional is most effective—a killer first sentence, then support, and a zinger ending. Maybe though, your writer finds a new rhythm by shaking out one sentence into the next. Link sentences by words (repeat key words), or images (extend a metaphor). Now's the time to look at how she uses all her tools (words, syntax, register, and so on) to weave the text together in order to tie down a reader's attention.

Before revising in, perhaps the writer rigorously revised out, writing too many comparisons and analogies and taking too many side trips. Ask the writer to survey the landscape, to catalog the ones she has and select: Which is most useful for her purposes? Which seems newest? Like any seasoning, try to figure out how much is too much, how much is just right. Read aloud. Listen to the shape and selection. You both can hear what is going on. Then articulate it so it can go on again in the next text, helping your writer to concentrate by internalizing these skills.

Highlighting and dramatizing   We live in the brave new world of webs. Don't forget that mixing genres helps add interest and that the tools and techniques of the technical writer and web composer are out there for the borrowing—in small doses. As in dress and hair color, we need to match effect to occasion. But here's where your writer starts thinking more of audience/reader.

- For instance, wouldn't a bullet list let each question stand out, helping my future reader find her way?

Midway through drafting this chapter I knew I would come back and try to help you out with new formatting. It's fun to run on draft ideas. But I owe it to you to help you through the thicket. So I can bullet or diamond list. I can italicize and clip art and hypertext. But remember, this is all coming after the fact. If my process has worked, I've said something and now I want to make you feel it like I feel it. I don't want my drama to stand in for substance (it won't, never fooled anyone that way), but I do like using it to help you find your readerly way and hear my writerly voice. There. Here. The same holds true for you and the writer in a tutorial.

Editing and Proofing

The two tricks I use most often in writing classes actually come from lessons I've learned in tutorial sessions and the desire to make writing more actively engaging.

Wall editing   I ask all writers in a class to stand (must not sit—leads to sleepiness) and read the text aloud and make first corrections. Tutors and tutees have long read to and for each other. But try this. Foolishness wakes us up. Have your writer stand and read aloud to the wall and you can quietly take notes of things you might mention later. Before you do mention them, the writer will have heard/seen/found several spots to talk about.

Swap editing   Edit someone else, but only off-text (only the author marks on the text). In group tutorials, this can lead to small group discussions. Why did this writer place a comma after all conjunctions (*and, or, so, for, but, yet*) and this writer didn't? Just what is the convention anyway?

About this time, I imagine you are saying, What's so creative about this? This is tutoring? My response: Exactly!

Georgia Heard writes, "At a recent workshop I asked people to list where poems hide in their lives. Here are some of the places they named: in my father's chair, in spider webs attached to the walls of the garage, in the taste of spinach in my mouth, in my mother's silence."[6] And here I'll borrow again. Where do the texts your students bring to you in writing centers really come from? Where do they hide in their lives? Ask this of them actively, and those texts will arrive and begin to grow.

I think active tutoring, collaborative discussions of writing progress, concentrated periods for attention to texts, creates space for creativity and engagement in writing. Writer and reader are always co-creating meaning in a text. From my point of view, it's essential that tutors be practicing writers—that means sometimes basic writers and sometimes wildly successful writers—but most often living somewhere in between. (Note: I can make anyone a basic writer. Here's your assignment: In five minutes, write a Shakespearean sonnet.) The more you try out these techniques, the more you'll be able to help the client you work with tailor them to the current tutoring situation. That means, too, collecting a few books on writing, like those listed in this chapter and throughout this collection.

That also means, read rhetorically and read for style, all the time, whenever you can. By analyzing the styles of writing you encounter in the world you'll become a more proficient brainstormer and adviser to your clients on the options available to them. Let's face it. We don't look the same, dress the same. Why should our prose? Then, put all these bits of advice in service of helping the writers you work with interrogate convention and experimentation as tandem parts of the writing process. Without one, there's not the other. Without the convention of workplace dress codes, dress down Friday means nothing. Without mystery and romance writing, literary genres have no backdrop and no way to achieve a false sense of superiority. And vice versa. Without carefully constructing the lab report, plunging into research writing, or digging in and taking a strong position, the college student is only partially educated in the conventions of the academy, no matter how many impressionistic and self-satisfying poems he writes late at night in the dorm. Not either/or but both/and.

Complicating Matters

Well, I can raise some arguments for you. Since I'm just finishing drafting, you can't possibly raise them for yourselves.

You: I'm faced with a student who wants a paper fixed and doesn't care about drafting out and drafting in. He wants to draft done.

Me: That's why I acknowledged that some of these tries won't result in a better immediate text. This is a matter of philosophy—mine, yours, that of the center you work in. For me, it's important to help the student to experience writing as a writer and to get further along on the path of lifelong literacy. I understand there are many other philosophies and many other daily forces at work on the tutoring scene, but this is always my tacit if not my explicit stance. I don't mind being dual: tutoring for the conventions and tutoring unconventionally, because I think this is how we learn best, as writers.

You: I don't like to write all that much, as much as you're suggesting. I'm a good editor and that's proved to be what most of my clients want to hear about from me.

Me: Maybe I'm a little evangelical here but I do believe writing is one of the best ways to improve any lot in life—to learn how to think more deeply, to understand the self better, to work out problems, to clarify beliefs, and to evaluate experiences. I'd ask you to do both/and here. Don't give up your pride in your editing and don't fail to please your clients with those skills but do notice how you may be improving as a writer through the act of tutoring and writing with your client and how those skills are equally to be valued. Then write some more. (There, I can't help but be evangelical.)

You: Tutorials go by too fast for these activities. You don't understand my writing center situation . . .

Me: I do realize all my suggestions have to be adapted to local contexts. But also I do write from an understanding of contemporary theory and research into writing and reading that suggests there are commonalities of process and purpose that undergird all acts of composing. I've tried to draw from that research, to make suggestions that can be tailored to tutorial, client, and center in ways that are helpful. You are the expert here—start from what you know. But just as a writer must start into new territory at many points in a drafting process, consider what you can learn from some of these new (if they are new to you) techniques and attitudes toward tutoring.

My sense is this—if you look to the invention-based exercises found in some of the books listed next, you'll discover writing prompts that will engage you. You'll try them and you'll like the results of some of those tries. You'll enter the next tutorial with an experience-based enthusiasm that lets you recommend similar activities to your clients. You'll both be engaged. You'll both be creative. You'll both be learning about writing—at the same time—for the day's text, for texts in the future. Writers write. Positive writing experiences make more writing. There's a math metaphor around here waiting to be thrown in—something about compound interest and exponential growth when you have a writer in the house, when you and your client are both writers in the writing center. But I'm going to throw in the towel instead, and let you take that last step yourself.

Further Reading

Behn, Robin, and Chase Twichell, eds. 1992. *The Practice of Poetry: Writing Exercises from Poets Who Teach.* New York: HarperPerennial.

Practicing poets suggest guided inventions: starting poems; focusing on image and metaphor; exploring self and subject; shaping inventions into forms; exploring sound and line; and experimenting with revision. Tutors will enjoy reading the sample poems and suggestions for further reading.

Bernays, Anne, and Pamela Painter. 1995. *What If? Writing Exercises for Fiction Writers.* New York: HarperCollins.

Here is a sourcebook of invention exercises such as "journey of the long sentence" and "practice writing good, clean prose"; the text encourages writers to become more involved with their drafts and includes samples of completed exercises by students.

Elbow, Peter, and Pat Belanoff. 1995. *Sharing and Responding*. 2d ed. New York: McGraw-Hill.

What to say about a piece of writing? The authors offer alternative response methods for readers, writers, conferencing, workgroups and workshops, as well as suggestions for helping writers share work and perform descriptive, analytic, reader-based, and criterion-based responses.

Goldberg, Natalie. 1990. *Wild Mind: Living the Writer's Life*. New York: Bantam.

This book offers sixty-two writer-, workgroup-, and workshop-related narrative discussions, most with a suggested exercise; it includes general writing topics and focuses on helping writers to improve their writing habits.

Notes

1. Brewster Ghiselin, *The Creative Process* (New York: Mentor/Penguin, 1952), 113.
2. Susan Wyche, "Time, Tools, Talismans," in *The Subject Is Writing: Essays by Teachers and Students,* 2d ed., ed. Wendy Bishop (Portsmouth, NH: Boynton/Cook, 1999), 32.
3. Wyche, 33.
4. Michael Walters, "Auction: First Lines," in *The Practice of Poetry: Writing Exercises from Poets Who Teach,* eds. Robin Behn and Chase Twichell (New York: HarperPerennial, 1992), 15.
5. Peter Elbow and Pat Belanoff, *Sharing and Responding,* 2d ed. (New York: McGraw-Hill, 1995), 16.
6. Georgia Heard, *Writing Toward Home* (Portsmouth, NH: Heinemann, 1995), 11.

Works Cited

Bishop, W., ed. 1997. *Elements of Alternate Style: Essays on Writing and Revision*. Portsmouth, NH: Boynton/Cook.

———. 1998. *Released into Language: Options for Teaching Creative Writing*. 2d ed. Portland, ME: Calendar Islands.

Elbow, P. 1993. "Ranking, Evaluating, and Liking: Sorting Out Three Forms of Judgment." *College English* 55: 187–206.

Ghiselin, B. 1952. *The Creative Process*. New York: Mentor/Penguin.

Goldberg, N. 1986. *Writing Down the Bones: Freeing the Writer Within*. Boston: Shambhala.

Heard, G. 1995. *Writing Toward Home*. Portsmouth, NH: Heinemann.

Hughes, E. F. 1991. *Writing from the Inner Self*. New York: HarperPerennial.

Murray, D. 1991. "All Writing Is Autobiography." *College Composition and Communication* 42: 66–74.

Ostrom, H., W. Bishop, and K. Haake. 2000. *Metro: Journeys in Writing Creatively*. New York: Longman.

Reigstad, T. J., and D. McAndrew. 1984. *Training Tutors for Writing Center Confer-ences.* Urbana, IL: NCTE.

Walters, M. 1992. "Auction: First Lines." In *The Practice of Poetry: Writing Exercises from Poets Who Teach,* eds. R. Behn and C. Twichell, 15–16. New York: Harper-Perennial.

Wyche, S. 1999. "Time, Tools, Talismans." In *The Subject Is Writing: Essays by Teach-ers and Students,* 2d ed., ed. W. Bishop, 30–42. Portsmouth, NH: Boynton/Cook.

10

A Balancing Act of Efficiency and Exploration

Tutoring Writers in Advanced Classes

Pavel Zemliansky

Even the most creative and enthusiastic writers have moments when they just wish they could finish a piece of writing and forget about it. Having observed upper-division students for several years now, I have noticed that this attitude is more common among them than it is for first-year students, who tend to be more receptive to the new learning experiences that college offers. Students in majors classes often require a different approach than the one tutors might use for first-year students because they tend to see their writing assignments as only marginally necessary. In their minds, writing is located outside of the process of learning the subject matter of their discipline. What matters most to them, it often seems, is learning about their majors through the process of reading textbooks, listening to lectures, and taking tests. Writing occupies the fringes of this process, a necessary albeit tedious chore.

Writing center tutors may encounter two related problems when working with students in advanced classes. First, tutors may be unfamiliar with the specialized discourse these students use in their papers, and second, tutors may be unprepared to deal with these students' insistence on following the most efficient route to completing the writing assignment even as they resist the tutor's advice to explore ideas.

I believe it is our duty as writing center tutors to help all writers not only communicate effectively through the conventions of academic discourse, but also to help them rediscover (or discover for the first time, in some cases) the learning and exploratory potential of writing. In this chapter, I focus on why this is especially important for students in advanced undergraduate classes and what tutors can do to achieve it.

Some Background

As writing center tutors know, most first-year, required college composition classes teach writing as a rhetorical process of exploration and learning. Students are given multiple opportunities for revision, for receiving feedback from their peers and instructors, and for verbalizing their writing strategies and behaviors. In other words, writing is taught not just as a skill to be mastered but also as a tool for thinking and learning. Very often this type of instruction in introductory college composition classes clashes with the notions of writing students inherit from their secondary schools. Many first-year composition teachers, myself included, work hard to "unteach" students' unproductive or outdated ideas about writing such as insistence on five-paragraph themes, excessive attention to mechanics, and little attention to content.

When students leave first-year composition classes, they often face a situation that is vastly different from what they experienced in their first-year writing courses. When they write for courses in the disciplines, they face a world of diverse disciplinary discourses. In other words, when they write they are expected to use the language, format, and style that professionals in their field use. It is usually not acceptable, for example, for a chemistry major to write a lab report in the discourse of a persuasive essay, a research paper, or a marketing analysis. While there may be overlap between discourses—using narrative in English and in archaeology, for example—students must learn the discourse of their discipline, and this usually occurs in their majors courses. As their commitments mount and courses grow more challenging, upper-level students also feel pressure to complete their writing quickly and efficiently, often without a chance for revision or feedback from their peers and the instructor. Instructors in upper-level courses may actually discourage peer feedback with warnings about cheating and plagiarism, and some may be less willing than first-year composition instructors to provide feedback. That's because, in their opinion, they have time only for subject matter, not writing instruction, and students are supposed to learn how to write in the first-year composition course. For many students, this means a lack of discipline-specific writing instruction, coupled with having to write under intense pressure and without feedback or the chance to revise. The effect is often a significant shift in students' writing philosophies. Just when many of them had begun to see composing as a tool of exploration as well as communication in their first year of college, they are forced back into product-oriented writing. When such writers come to writing centers for help, these problems become visible to their tutors, who often do not know how to deal with them.

Students Writing in the Disciplines: Two Cases

About two years ago, when I was working as a writing center tutor in a large public university, I met two such students, Joe and Lynn. The center served a variety of students, from first-year to graduate, and did not have specialist tutors.

Joe was a sophomore environmental science major with a strong interest in his discipline. Joe and I worked together three times over a period of one week. The assignment that Joe brought with him to the writing center was from an introductory environmental science class, where students had been asked to analyze two pieces of state legislation dealing with conservation efforts in the Florida Everglades National Park and to develop a policy statement on the subject.

Joe was a fairly good writer; his paper was focused and reasonably well developed. He was also passionate about the subject of his writing and was able to explain to me, his nonspecialist tutor, some of the finer points of Florida's environmental legislation and how it applied to his project. At the end of the week, we both felt that our work in the writing center was not in vain.

The following week, I worked with Lynn, a senior majoring in computer science and writing a long term paper for one of her classes. It was a highly specialized piece of writing, involving complex theories from mathematics, physics, and even psychology. It was also full of references to specialized literature. I understood very little of Lynn's argument, but, worse still, Lynn seemed to be as confused as I was about what she was trying to do in the paper.

From the very start, Lynn and I ran into problems. Not only was her subject matter completely new to me, but our approaches to the composing process seemed to be vastly different. While I tried to get Lynn to write and revise multiple drafts (she had some time before the paper was due) and advised her to seek feedback from her professor, she resisted and told me that she could not show the paper to anyone before it was absolutely perfect. I tried to ask the usual clarifying questions about her purpose, audience, and the conventions of writing in her discipline. I sensed that Lynn was not used to talking about her writing with others, let alone to others who were not specialists in her discipline. We met two or three times, but, after our last session, Lynn's paper was still unfinished, and I don't believe she understood what to do with the paper any better than when she came into the writing center for the first time.

Writing center tutors who work with upper-division students have probably been in similar situations. I was able to help Joe more than Lynn for two reasons. First, Joe's subject matter and his rhetorical task were simpler than Lynn's because the argument he was trying to make was accessible by a nonspecialist reader like myself. Joe's writing philosophy and mine were more or less the same. Joe did not resist revision and was willing to seek feedback on his drafts. He was also passionate about his subject. Lynn, on the other hand, not only resisted what I considered to be sound composing practices but also did not seem to have any real interest in completing the paper beyond fulfilling a class requirement.

Generalist Versus Specialist Tutors: Advantages and Disadvantages

At least part of the solution to the problem of convincing upper-level students to become more engaged in their writing would seem to be to hire and train enough specialist tutors who are familiar with complex disciplinary discourses. However, this method has been tried by many writing centers, and often with disappointing results.[1] Moreover, hiring and training enough specialized tutors to accommodate the many needs students have is impractical and costly. Relying on specialized tutors may also lead to a disciplinary "fracturing" of the writing center, causing scheduling and other logistical problems. More important, however, the specialized-tutor approach may be detrimental to the fulfillment of the writing center's goals and to the student writers' progress.

Let me explain. Students who write in the disciplines tend to receive their assignments and discuss their writing only with people within their own disciplines, usually their professors. While such a practice is no doubt useful for learning discipline-specific writing conventions, it can also lead to a somewhat narrow view of writing. For example, a student who writes papers only on engineering for engineering classes and talks about them only to other engineers will not be able to develop the kind of rhetorical sensitivity and attention to the needs of diverse audiences as someone who produces a variety of discourses and shares them with diverse audiences both in and outside his own academic discipline. While such a practice can lead to better papers for a specific class, it will hardly help the writer's overall competence. What I am saying here, then, is that advanced writers need to get out of their disciplinary shells from time to time and write for a variety of purposes and audiences, and in a variety of contexts. Working with tutors from diverse backgrounds, academic disciplines, and approaches to writing will help achieve that goal.

It is important for tutors to understand that there are various perspectives on this issue, so let's examine this further. Kristin Walker provides insight into the complexity of the problem. According to Walker, some scholars, like Kiedaisch and Dinitz, Tinberg and Cupples, Shamoon and Burns, "argue that tutors' knowledge of discipline-specific discourse conventions is important for the success of tutoring sessions, since tutoring should revolve around the rhetoric of the discipline."[2] Other scholars argue that generalist tutors are better suited to help writers in the disciplines since they can help them to learn the conventions of their disciplines rather than "prematurely suggesting ways to revise the paper, based on his/her experience in the field."[3] Walker further cites authors who argue that generalist tutors can provide their clients with the opportunity to work with someone outside of their fields. This interaction, she states, allows generalist tutors to contribute feedback different from that offered by insiders to the discipline.[4] For example, a generalist tutor might ask advanced writers questions that would force them to verbalize their writing strategies, including ways by which they solve discipline-specific problems during composing. The writers would then become more aware of their composing processes and would be able to apply what they learned in the writing center in future writing situations.

Kathryn Evans provides a counterpoint to this view. She states that "it is unrealistic to expect a tutor to be familiar with all the conventions in all the disciplines."[5] Evans proposes two solutions to the problem. First, she argues that writing center tutors can help advanced writers become aware of the conventions of their own discipline by helping them understand both the general conventions of effective writing (such as rhetorical situation, appropriateness of style, and so on) and the specific conventions of their discipline. With this first solution, Evans seeks a middle ground between those who would prefer to have specialist tutors and those who would prefer generalists.

Evans' second solution is for writing center staff to work with professors in various disciplines. Specifically, Evans recommends that writing center staff ask professors to include tutors in the audience for writing assignments and to write better descriptions of the assignments that they give to their students.[6] According to Evans, assignments given to students by instructors in their disciplines often do not articulate the conventions of the discipline, thus leaving students confused and frustrated.[7]

Writing centers have tried other ways to solve the problem of helping writers in advanced classes. Many of these efforts begin (as they should) with an attempt to learn more about the kinds of writing students are asked to do in their classes. One such study was conducted by Kelly Faulkner and Francien Rohrbacher at California State University at Northridge. They designed a survey that asked faculty on their campus to describe their writing assignments as well as their expectations of writing center tutors. The survey showed that most faculty were concerned about what they saw as deteriorating writing skills among their students, which typically meant bad grammar. The survey also showed that "many faculty did not spend time explaining the writing process expected from students, and sometimes they didn't use written prompts either, expecting students to copy assignments written on the board."[8]

Taking a very practical approach to solving the problem and guided by the results of the survey, Faulkner and Rohrbacher created a handbook for writing center tutors that outlined the requirements for writing and discourse conventions in different disciplines. According to the authors, their tutors were initially skeptical about using the handbook, but they then realized its usefulness both as a time-saving and an illustrative device. Having the handbook allowed tutors to prepare themselves for their appointments with students by knowing in advance about the writing assignments and any specialized requirements their students were facing.

Practical solutions similar to the one described by Faulkner and Rohrbacher are, no doubt, helpful. Training writing center tutors to recognize the particulars of different disciplinary discourses will certainly help the center to conduct more productive and efficient tutoring sessions. However, I would like to argue that these practical steps are not sufficient if we are to help students to understand that good writing goes well beyond following a set of rules in a handbook or fulfilling a set of requirements for a class. In order to achieve the bigger goal of the writing center, which is to prepare independent writers familiar with the conventions of academic discourse, we need to reinforce in them a view of writing that is exploratory, experimental, and adventuresome. Heavy teaching loads as well as the need to teach large

amounts of subject matter in their courses prevent many instructors from paying sufficient attention to the teaching of writing. Consequently, students
become accustomed to seeing writing as a "necessary evil," a chore that must
be done as quickly and as efficiently as possible. Our goal as writing center
tutors should be to change this attitude. We need to help students see writing
as an essential part of learning.

What to Do

Recently, I taught a class on writing style to a group of juniors and seniors
from a variety of academic majors. Before each class session, many students
chatted about the kinds of writing they were working on in other classes. One
student, a political science major, was writing a long term paper, and every
time she came to my class, she wanted to tell everyone how much she had written the night before and how much more she still had to write. It got to the
point that when she entered the classroom, other students asked, "How many
pages do you have left to write, Joanne?" Joanne was good student and a good
writer. I am sure she did well with her political science paper and received a
good grade for it. However, what struck me was that she talked about her writing in terms of structure, in terms of length, and in terms of fulfilling a necessary but unpleasant chore, rather than how well the paper fulfilled the assignment or reached its intended audience. Discussions of her interest in the topic
of the paper or of what she was learning from the experience of writing it were
also absent.

     While it's only natural to want to finish a piece of writing and move on to
the next thing we have to do in our busy schedules, it is vital to remember that
writing assignments are meant for learning. The ultimate challenge for writing
center tutors working with writers in upper-division classes is not to help them
finish, or to write better papers for their classes. It is not even to help them
understand the discourse conventions of their chosen academic discipline.
These are all tools of the trade and they are only as good as the purpose to
which they are applied. The ultimate challenge is to prepare students to use
writing as a means of learning and to face a variety of writing situations on
their own.

     That a clash of approaches to writing exists between writing centers on
the one hand and instructors and students in the disciplines on the other has
been acknowledged most famously by Stephen North.

> In a writing center the object is to make sure that writers, and not necessar-
> ily their texts, are what get changed by instruction. In axiom form it goes like
> this: Our job is to produce better writers, not better writing. Any given
> project—a class assignment, a law school application letter, an encyclopedia
> entry, a dissertation proposal—is for the writer the prime, often the exclusive
> concern. That particular text, its success or failure is what brings them to talk

to us in the first place. In the center, though, we look beyond or through that particular project, that particular text, and see it as an occasion for addressing our primary concern, the process by which it is produced.[9]

North goes on to say that writing centers should serve the students and not academic curricula, which means that the primary goal of writing center tutors should not be to make sure that their clients get better grades in their classes but to ensure they learn something about writing. Teaching students to understand and apply conventions of discourse in their disciplines, it seems to me, is helpful only to a point. As writing center tutors, we must measure our success by the extent to which we combine instruction in academic discourse with the more ambitious task of changing our students' philosophies and attitudes about writing itself.

I would like to offer several suggestions to writing center tutors aimed at designing a strategy for working with writers from advanced classes. In offering these suggestions, I am guided by the premise that the goal of tutoring these writers is much more than helping them to write a good paper for a class or to understand the conventions of discourse in their field. The overarching goal of every tutoring session should be to help students assume an active and creative stance toward writing itself, to learn to see composing as a tool of learning and thinking, and not only a means of getting a good grade in a class. If we can achieve this overreaching goal, the good grades and the discourse conventions will follow.

Readers will notice that my suggestions are based on the overall principles and practices of sound one-on-one tutoring. I am building on the theory and practice of writing center work already accepted by the majority of tutors, adding to it, and fine-tuning it to meet the needs of writers from advanced classes. Taking these steps will help these writers become more aware of their disciplinary discourses, but, more important, it will lead them to rediscover, or discover for the first time, the power of writing to promote exploration and learning.

Because you are working with writers from upper-level courses, what you do during your session with them will probably be somewhat different from what you do when tutoring a first-year writer. I try to address the differences between the two tutoring situations in each of the following suggestions as much as possible. At the same time, as a tutor, you should remember that the foundations of writing center work are the same, regardless of the experience or the proficiency of the student seated with you at the conference table.

Suggestion 1: Begin by Discussing the Whole Assignment

Begin by discussing the writing assignment with the student, as you would in any tutoring session. Ask the student for a written copy of the assignment. If the assignment is not available in writing, create one from the student's oral description. Verbalizing the task will help the writer to better understand his

purpose and intended audience for the project because he will be required, perhaps for the first time, to see the assignment not simply as a class hoop to jump
through, but as a rhetorical problem. (See Chapter 1.)

Next, steer the discussion of the assignment toward rhetorical concepts
and concerns, such as purpose, intended audience, and context and constraints.
For example, you may want to ask the writer to explain the purpose and the
audience for the assignment, the way she sees it, as well as any requirements
for the length, style, and format of the paper.

When discussing the rhetorical context for the assignment, consider disciplinary and practical concerns. For instance, draw the writer's attention to
how the project fits into any ongoing discussions or debates in his field. Try
to get the writer to think about the ways in which the topic for the paper fits
(or does not fit) into that discussion. Of course, this point becomes less relevant if the topic is assigned by the professor. But even in that case, it is
extremely important for the student writer to realize why he undertakes the
writing project and how this work fits into the ongoing conversation in
the field. Next, ask the student what constitutes legitimate evidence in the
writer's discipline. For example, can the writer support his thesis by quoting
another author's opinion, or is it necessary to find and cite a research study
for evidence? Also discuss what writing styles and voices seem to be accepted
and preferred.

Now is also a good time to talk about the expectations of the instructor
who assigned the paper. Because the instructor is a part of the audience who
sets the parameters for writing, her preferences in reading and evaluating the
piece need to be considered. When discussing the instructor's reading style
and preferences, tutors need to be careful not to create the impression in the
student that she is working for the instructor alone. Emphasize that the instructor is only one member of the audience for the paper and that when reading the
paper, the instructor is guided (or should be guided, at least) by how well the
assignment fulfills its rhetorical purpose and adheres to the broad discourse
conventions of the academic discipline.

Writing center tutors can help their clients see writing not as an isolated
act aimed only at receiving a grade, but as a contribution to the professional
conversation in their field. Tutors can accomplish this by helping writers to
identify the immediate audience and context of the paper (usually the class
and instructor), as well as the broader purposes, audiences, and implications
of the piece.

Suggestion 2: Ask Questions

Every tutoring session is an act of collaboration. After helping the student to
understand her purpose and intended audience for the assignment (and after
learning about them yourself), the next step is to go through the draft with the
writer, asking for clarifications on the subject matter of the paper. Ask

questions, especially if you are reading a highly specialized discourse with which you are not familiar. At this point, the writer may object to this strategy by saying that in her academic or professional community, everyone would know what the paper is talking about and so additional explanations are not necessary. This may be true, and the writer must decide this for herself. But point out that the practice of explaining difficult concepts and arguments to an outside audience like you can help the writer to identify places where an inside or specialized audience might also need additional explanations and clarifications.

Suggestion 3: Focus on the Writing Process

Get the student to verbalize his writing behavior and strategies. I often like to ask my upper-division writing students to speak about the differences between academic discourses in the different classes they are taking. Ask the student to think about how discourse is constructed in her discipline and why it is constructed that way. Discuss purpose, audience, common writing styles, and so on. A useful strategy to help advanced writers understand the differences has been suggested, among others, by Irene L. Clark, who points out that in the past, the term *genre* was defined and discussed in terms of form and structure. Clark writes that "the most notorious example of this approach is the paradigm of the five-paragraph essay, which many students apply indiscriminately to any writing task they are asked to complete. . . . "[10] She further notes that, in recent literature, *genre* is discussed as a concept of function or motive, and that this new understanding of genre has great pedagogical potential. She argues that this new definition of genre, which is connected with social-constructivist rhetoric, offers writing teachers and tutors ways to teach academic and professional discourses as rhetorical and intellectual constructs rather than forms.[11] This new understanding also allows writers and their teachers to see any writing situation in rhetorical terms. Rather than arbitrarily applying a set of generic and formal rules to a piece of writing, students will be able to see the papers they write for classes in different disciplines as representations of genres that these disciplines use. Obviously, to apply Clark's model to tutoring advanced writers, we need to make the discussion of disciplinary conventions and the differences between discourses of different fields a central concept in our work.

In my experience as a writing center tutor and as a teacher of advanced writing classes, most upper-division students are proficient users of standard written English, so, in most cases, you will not have to teach them basic grammar. What many upper-level students do have problems with is applying the appropriate writing style to a text. For example, one senior political science major recently told me that he prides himself on his writing in political science where he feels in control, competent, and consistently receives good grades. At the same time, that student was often at a loss when writing for the classes outside of his major because he was unsure whether the writing style he had developed for writing about political science would fit other rhetorical situations. Often, this is a matter of the writer's confidence as much as of rhetorical prowess. Tutors of such students should not only encourage them to follow the discourses and writing styles of their disciplines, but also to experiment with new styles, approaches, and writing techniques.

Suggestion 4: Treat Citation of Sources Rhetorically

Teach citation and documentation standards as rhetorical devices. As Chris Anson writes,

> Most college-level instruction in how to incorporate outside sources into an original paper focuses on concerns that lie at the surface of the writer's text: deciding whether to quote material directly, paraphrase it, or summarize it; knowing when to use block quotations; choosing the appropriate reference style and following its conventions for source attribution. Although these general skills are important for much documented writing, they are also insufficient. Students need experience with the more complex "deep structures" of source work—including its rhetorical and informational purposes.[12]

According to Anson, such work includes evaluating sources for their worth and the *sophistication of evidence* presented in them, deciding whether the audience will accept the source in the same way the writer does, and so on. Finally, it is important to help student writers see whole systems of documentation accepted in their disciplines as rhetorical devices designed to fulfill a rhetorical purpose. Such an approach may help the student see citation and documentation conventions not only as tools of efficiency and authority, but also of rhetoric, learning, and exploration. In this chapter, for example, I cited Anson's work in part to show that I am a credible writer who can back up what I say. At the same time, rereading Anson's work pointed me to other sources that helped me to write another section of this chapter.

Suggestion 5: Be Realistic About Student Resistance

What to do when a student resists? As has been stated many times in writing center literature, there is simply no short-term solution for this problem when it is rooted in a looming deadline. By giving in to the student's demands to help her "fix" the paper, which is due just hours later, we would be doing such a student a disservice, and all tutors and writing center administrators realize that. I would like to argue that solving this problem will take a campuswide redefinition of the goals and purposes of writing and methods to get it done. As we discuss our work and our hopes with the professors in the disciplines and university administrators, we can begin to effect such change through our conversations with advanced students, one student at a time. There is nothing wrong with telling a student writer demanding a quick fix of a paper that there is nothing that you, as a tutor, can do for her (but see Chapter 4 for suggestions on how to engage reluctant writers). Of course, tutors will need to make sure that they are on the same page with their writing center's policy on this issue. Providing writing center tutors with practical handbooks of the kind described in the article by Faulkner and Rohrbacher, cited earlier, is only a short-term solution. Teaching tutors to recognize and understand conventions of disciplinary discourse will work better in conjunction with the steps outlined in this chapter.

Suggestion 6: Reach out to Other Tutors and Teachers

Discuss the needs of your students with other writing center tutors and, whenever possible, with instructors in various disciplines. If your college or university has a writing-across-the-curriculum or writing-in-the-disciplines program, and if you have any kind of access to people who either teach in that program or administer it, use that access to network and to inform others in different departments about the goals, objectives, and methods of the writing center. Such networking will help the students, the instructors, and the writing center tutors. Advanced writing students will benefit from an increased sense of collaboration and a unified and concerted effort from all interested participants to improve writing instruction. Most of this work will probably be done by writing center directors and other administrators. However, you, as a tutor, can do your part to change the campuswide attitudes about writing.

Some of the challenges that writing center tutors encounter when working with advanced writers are unique, and some are the same as the ones you will face while tutoring first-year students. The work of the writing center should contribute to the sense of continuity in students' understanding of their development as writers and learners. Writing centers can become sites where the differences in the kinds of writing assignments that students receive in their various academic classes are explored, explained, and understood. Helping advanced student writers to piece together all of their writing experiences, assignments, successes, and failures into one whole should be among the goals and purposes of writing centers. By encouraging reflection and active questioning, we can help advanced students both master the conventions of academic discourse as well as balance efficiency with learning and exploration. I end with a quote from Maxine Hairston: "To help students grow, [writing teachers] must find ways to encourage them to take risks . . . most people do not write well when they are afraid; they cannot use their abilities fully when they are on the defensive, trying to play it safe."[13] As writing tutors, we are at least partially responsible for helping students overcome the fear of taking risks in their writing.

Further Reading

Boquet, Elizabeth. 2002. *Noise from the Writing Center*. Logan: Utah State University Press.

Boquet argues that writing centers should be "noisy" and open to the often-unpredictable nature of writing and learning. Such an atmosphere will encourage the kind of creativity and risk-taking that supports tutors who work with students in upper-division classes.

Flynn, Thomas, and Mary King, eds. 1993. *Dynamics of the Writing Conference: Social and Cognitive Interaction*. Urbana, IL: NCTE.

The contributors to this collection cover cognitive and rhetorical aspects of the one-on-one writing conference. The book includes examples of student writing and case studies. Learning about the approaches and strategies proposed by the contributors will help writing center tutors better understand unique challenges of working with upper-level writing.

Nelson, Jane, and Kathy Evertz, eds. 2001. *The Politics of Writing Centers*. Portsmouth, NH: Boynton/Cook.

The authors examine the place of writing centers as potential sites of conflict and of various political struggles within university and college communities. The book is useful for tutors and administrators who work with students from various disciplines and who are interested in a cross-disciplinary approach to writing center work.

Pemberton, Michael, and Joyce Kinkead, eds. 2003. *The Center Will Hold: Critical Perspectives on Writing Center Scholarship*. Logan: Utah State University Press.

This award-winning collection of essays discusses theoretical and pedagogical issues surrounding the work of writing center tutors. The contributors include teachers of composition, English, technical writing, and other disciplines. Their cross-disciplinary approaches will be of interest to tutors who work with writers from various academic disciplines and backgrounds.

Notes

1. Kelly Faulkner and Francien Rohrbacher, "A Writing Center Facilitates Student Writing Across the Curriculum," *Academic Exchange Quarterly* 7 (1) (2003): 174–77.

2. Kristin Walker, "The Debate over Generalist and Specialist Tutors: Genre Theory's Contribution," *Writing Center Journal* 18 (2) (1998): 27.

3. Walker, 27–28.

4. Walker, 27.

5. Kathryn Evans, "Problems in the Writing Center," *Academic Exchange Quarterly* 7 (1) (2003): 261.

6. Evans, 260–61.

7. Evans, 262–63.

8. Faulkner and Rohrbacher, 277.

9. Stephen North, "The Idea of the Writing Center," *College English* 46 (5) (1984): 437.

10. Irene L. Clark, "Addressing Genre in the Writing Center," *Writing Center Journal* 20 (1) (1999): 8.

11. Clark, 10–11.

12. Chris Anson, "Citation as Speech Act: Exploring the Pragmatics of Reference," in eds., Pavel Zemliansky and Wendy Bishop, *Research Writing Revisited: A Sourcebook for Teachers* (Portsmouth, NH: Heinemann, 2004), 203.

13. Maxine Hairston, "Working with Advanced Writers," *College Composition and Communication* 35 (2) (1984): 205.

Works Cited

Anson, C. 2004. "Citation as Speech Act: Exploring the Pragmatics of Reference." In *Research Writing Revisited: A Sourcebook for Teachers,* eds. P. Zemliansky and W. Bishop, 203–13. Portsmouth, NH: Heinemann.

Clark, I. L. 1999. "Addressing Genre in the Writing Center." *Writing Center Journal* 20 (1): 7–32.

Evans, K. 2003. "Problems in the Writing Center." *Academic Exchange Quarterly* 7 (1): 261–68.

Faulkner, K., and F. Rohrbacher. 2003. "A Writing Center Facilitates Student Writing Across the Curriculum." *Academic Exchange Quarterly* 7 (1): 174–77.

Hairston, M. 1984. "Working with Advanced Writers." *College Composition and Communication* 35 (2): 196–208.

North, S. 1984. "The Idea of a Writing Center." *College English* 46 (5): 433–46.

Walker, K. 1998. "The Debate over Generalist and Specialist Tutors: Genre Theory's Contribution." *Writing Center Journal* 18 (2): 27–46.

11

Organizing Ideas

Focus Is the Key

Alice L. Trupe

A week after my friend had moved into a great Victorian house, I visited her and found every dish unpacked and in the cupboard, every book, tape, and CD in alphabetical order on a shelf. It looked as though she'd lived there for years. "How do you do it?" I asked in amazement. "I can't concentrate on anything else until I've organized my space," she replied.

My office door opens on chaos every morning. Papers flow from my desk to a table, some overflowing onto the floor, CDs vie with coffee mugs for shelf space, and anyone trying to analyze my shelving system for books would be kept guessing a long time. I refer to this as creative chaos, and believe it or not, I can find any book or file when I need it! Does it look like organization? Not to other people, perhaps, but it works for me.

Organization in writing works like this. It comes down to whether the reader can find her way through it. Readers who can find their way believe the piece is well organized. Readers who lose their way say it's not; and since they cannot usually turn to the writer and ask, "Where's the stapler?" they often just give up or scrawl "org" in the margin of the students' papers. Tutors need to show writers where in the draft they become lost or confused and why; other times they need to help writers who don't yet have a draft to think of an organizational plan to get started. (See Chapter 8 for more on this.)

One student pulls two pages of lists from her backpack and tells a tutor, "I have lots of ideas, but I don't know where to get started." Another student hands the tutor a completed draft and asks for proofreading and editing help. The tutor finds that he can't follow the writer's thinking, that the focus seems to shift paragraph by paragraph and even within paragraphs. What strategies work best to support students whose papers seem to lack focus or whose paragraphs strike us as chaotic? What strategies help students find the key to organizing their ideas?

Some Background

Writing textbooks and handbooks generally recommend that student writers start with a thesis sentence, plan an outline, or cluster ideas.[1] Research into the practices and products of experienced writers, however, suggests that their plans and texts do not emerge the way that this advice suggests. Linda Flower and John Hayes' cognitive model of the writing process, based on analysis of talk-aloud protocols of writers as they composed, describes experienced writers' behaviors as directed by "a hierarchical network of goals."[2] As experienced writers compose, they generate and revise their goals, as well as translate content into words, through a process of discovery and recursion. Inexperienced writers, by contrast, tend to fall back on plans governed by the classroom assignment. Drawing on Flower and Hayes' findings, tutors can help inexperienced writers articulate specific goals for their writing tasks. As students coordinate their goals for affecting an audience with their thinking about the content, they establish their own guidelines for focus and organization.

Tutors may be surprised to learn that a review of the writing of established professional writers has revealed that organization is not a function of clearly defined topic sentences that control subordinate sentences. As Richard Braddock reports in his landmark article, "The Frequency and Placement of Topic Sentences in Expository Prose," fewer than half the paragraphs in twenty-five essays he examined had topic sentences at all.[3] Why, then, do so many writing texts continue to emphasize the outline and the topic sentence? The advice derives from Alexander Bain's 1866 *English Composition and Rhetoric,* as Francis Christensen points out. Christensen comments on the discrepancy between what composition instructors require student writers to do and what they themselves do as writers: "I doubt that many of us write many paragraphs the way we require our charges to write them or that we could find many paragraphs that exemplify the methods of development or the patterns of movement."[4]

Christensen also suggests that paragraphs develop from the topic sentence through "structurally related sentences,"[5] and he notes that a topic sentence does not always explicitly specify the thesis of the paragraph, that it may be a very short sentence or even a fragment, and that it may even be a question. The point is, he asserts, that the sentence should perform the function of orienting the reader. Similarly, Rich Eden and Ruth Mitchell advise that, since readers' interpretations of a text are shaped by the expectations raised at the beginning of paragraphs, paragraphs should be designed from the perspective of a reader rather than shaped by the context of what the writer must say.[6]

W. Ross Winterowd, another rhetorician, argues for a theory of paragraph development based on coherence. The structure of an essay involves transitional relationships between its parts, he believes.[7] Yet another rhetorician, Frank J. D'Angelo, "revisits" the topic sentence to rethink its usefulness in guiding readers through a text. Citing readability research, D'Angelo makes a qualified argument for the use of "a clearly defined organizational pattern . . . appropriately signaled to the reader."[8] While acknowledging that many texts by professional writers lack topic sentences, he asks us to consider whether those texts might be improved by their use.

Karen Burke LeFevre, who has enriched our understanding of focus and organization by emphasizing the social dimension of writing, observes that each act of invention occurs within a specific social and cultural context, reaffirming the point that writers need to have audience awareness in planning, composing, and revising. This renewed emphasis on audience and context, originating in classical rhetorical instruction, has been blended with the cognitive model in Linda Flower and her colleagues' later work, such as her 1994 book, *Making Thinking Visible*.

In short, the message for tutors is that the problem of establishing focus through a clear organizational pattern is best addressed by helping the writer to think through her goals for the text, instead of concentrating single-mindedly on meeting teacher explanations or getting everything she knows about the topic into an outline.

What to Do

For either the student who has lists of ideas but does not know where to begin or the student who is ready to revise but whose paper seems to lack a clear focus and structure, the task is twofold: Establish a governing purpose for the text, and organize the text to fulfill the writer's purpose.

Establishing a Focus for the Writing Task

Linda Flower recommends that the student writer "nutshell" her ideas, and this is a useful strategy for beginning discussion: "Tell me, in a nutshell, what your paper is about."[9] Alternatively, the tutor might ask the student to imagine a phone conversation with a parent, a sibling, or a friend back home in which she is telling that person what the paper is about. Another useful scenario involves imagining the paper as a brief email message: "What's the subject line? What can you say in two or three sentences that captures the entire paper in a nutshell?" Having a repertoire of strategies for capturing the gist of the paper is useful for working with writers in either the predrafting or revising phase.

But the writer may need to articulate his goals before getting to a nutshell version of the paper, and this may be especially useful for someone who has not yet started drafting. The way that this writer can establish a structure for his paper is to establish some goals for communicating with the reader. It can be beneficial for tutors to think theoretically about how writers develop goals. While I don't believe writers need to be taught this theory, it does give tutors a framework for understanding and talking about a nebulous but important aspect of teaching writing. In establishing goals, for example, the writer is doing more than creating an outline: he is creating principles to guide his process as well as his content. Think of these process goals as the instructions people give themselves like, "I want my ending to circle back to my introduction." As Flower and Hayes observe, "Good writers often give themselves many such instructions and seem to have greater conscious control over their own processes than the poorer writers we have studied."[10] They define content goals and plans as "all the things the writer wants to say or do to an audience," and they point out that goals for organization may specify both process and content, as in, "I want to open with a statement about political views."[11] Thus, by focusing the writer's attention on his goals for the paper rather than on a thesis and major points, a tutor may help the writer adopt more effective writing behaviors. And these behaviors can then result in ideas that are more thoroughly developed through a process of discovery. A writer may find it useful to freewrite about her purpose for five minutes or so before creating a tentative plan for the paper.

Planning Reader-Based Rather Than Writer-Based Texts

Some of the most effective growth writers experience comes from shifting their orientation from "What do I want to say?" to "What does the reader need to know?" To plan a reader-based text, tutors can help guide the writer to generate questions a reader might have about the topic. The writer can then draft the text as answers to those questions, revising the questions out of the text at a later stage. Tutors might help the writer to reenter one of the previous scenarios suggested—imagining a telephone conversation and what questions the caller might have, or imagining an e-mail exchange in which someone asks a series of questions based on the previous e-mail message that described the topic in two or three sentences.

An important consideration for tutors to bear in mind here is that while a question-based conversation may seem analogous to the journalist's five "W-questions," the approach I'm suggesting requires contextually based questions, that is, questions specifically connected to the writer's goals for the text. Reducing the questions to a formula like Who? What? Where? When? Why? may reduce the options the writer can imagine for developing her text by focusing all of her attention on telling what she knows, as I mentioned in the previous section.

When a writer has a completed draft that seems disorganized, establishing his goals for the paper may help in rethinking the organization. Articulating the paper's overall purpose in terms of how he wants readers to respond will aid in establishing a rhetorical purpose for deciding what should come first and what should follow each idea throughout the paper. The tutor who plays the role of naive reader by periodically posing questions framed in terms of reader expectations can be very helpful here: "When I read this sentence, it leads me to expect that you're going to talk about X, but then when I get to this sentence, it's not about X, it's about Y, so I feel lost."

Viewing a Confusing Paper as a Discovery Draft

In many cases, a reader has difficulty following a paper because it reflects what the writer thinks he is supposed to do rather than reflecting a rhetorical purpose of his own. Or perhaps the writer has simply transcribed all the information he had on the topic. Either way, the writer hasn't established her own purpose as a writer.

An apparently disorganized paper might actually be a discovery draft, although the student hasn't realized this and so comes to the writing center just to clean up his sentence structure and mechanics. While reading the draft, the tutor finds that the writer has "hit her stride" about midway through the paper, where voice and coherence seem to improve significantly. As a composition instructor, I often see this pattern in papers that students turn in to me. Or perhaps the writer has made her most important point midway through the paper but has retreated from it in attempting to match the conclusion to an introductory paragraph written days ago. In this case, the writer may have started with a very clear thesis statement and written a conclusion designed to match it, all the while overlooking the really important ideas that the writing process itself generated. Such a writer may benefit most from hearing a tutor say,

> Your most interesting point seems sort of buried in the next-to-last sentence of paragraph three. It's a good idea. I wonder if it might be easier for a reader to see its importance if you brought it out more. Could you add something to your intro that anticipates this great insight? Will that change your conclusion at all?

The tutor who values the writer's insights and helps her think about organizational patterns that bring them out can experience a tremendous sense of accomplishment.

A writer who discovers what he has to say only in his concluding paragraph will probably benefit most from writing a whole new draft. He, too, needs a tutor's assurance that he has generated good ideas in what he has done so far. The tutor can say,

> It seems to me that your final couple of paragraphs say some really interesting things, and the writing strikes me as stronger here. You could build a whole essay around what you've said here. What would happen if you just started your paper with these two paragraphs and went from there?

When tutors cannot recognize the student's intended organization, outlining the paper is a good first step. The tutor might say, "I think you have some really good ideas here, but I'm having a little difficulty seeing how they fit together. Could we make an outline to look more closely at your organization?"

Or mapping the main ideas and creating a visual representation of their relationships can aid the writer in revising for clearer organization. Outlining or mapping at this stage, face to face with a reader, the writer can better see the relationships she has and hasn't established between paragraphs and between sentences (see Chapter 1). As she analyzes her own text, she may discover other ways to support her goals for the paper. Remember, outlining need not lead to the creation of a topic sentence for each paragraph; it is, rather, a discovery tool, a technique for discovering what she has to say through looking at how she has said it. "How can I know what I mean until I see what I say?" is the question quoted by Flower, Murray, and other writing teachers.

Using Transitions to Clarify Organization

Using or omitting transitional wording can direct the writer's attention to organizational matters, as Winterowd recommends.[12] A tutor may ask the writer how each sentence relates to the sentence that precedes it and how each paragraph relates to the preceding paragraph. The tutor may help a visual thinker by using the term *signposting* and telling the writer, "Your reader needs directional signs when she arrives at a crossroads." Or the tutor may suggest potential relationships: "Is X an example of Y?" Some words and phrases for introducing examples are *for instance, for example, in some cases,* and so forth. With this technique, the writer may become better able to revise for organization on her own.

Complicating Matters

It would seem as though organization is simply a matter of creating readers' expectations and then fulfilling them, of being predictable. Is there anything wrong with this picture of good writing? Doesn't it sound a little boring? Surely, good writing is anything but boring!

Where's the room for the unexpected, for the surprising? Sometimes a writer's seemingly well-structured text is so predictable that even the reader who holds the grade book will find it boring. Can we encourage such a writer to back off from predictability? Instead of helping the writer to lay out the thesis sentence in the first paragraph, to follow through with several paragraphs headed by clear topic sentences, and to sum up the entire paper in the conclusion, we may need to help her complicate her own template for good writing.

Faced with a predictable text, the tutor might ask the student to talk about the kinds of texts he likes to read. Chances are that he will mention some popular fiction that captures readers with suspense. A tutor's response might be,

> What is it that you like about Mary Higgins Clark's writing? Are there some ways you can use her style of writing as a model for your own writing? Try thinking like Mary Higgins Clark. How would she write this paper?

Of course, we're going to temper this line of reasoning with some of the important differences between best-selling suspense novels and classroom writing assignments, but the student who has always divorced his writing from the reading he enjoys may profit from shifting his point of view and thinking of himself as a real *writer*. Students who rarely read for pleasure may especially benefit from this approach if it is expanded to include the song lyrics or the movies they enjoy.

Too often when we read we are blind to our own preconceptions as to what constitutes good organization. It's best to read student writers' texts with open minds. Asking ourselves—and the writer—"What is this writer trying to do here? What are the goals for this piece of writing?" may help us recognize unfamiliar organizational patterns where our preconceived ideas might have obscured the writer's purpose from us.[13]

We may encounter plans that reflect cultural patterns of discourse different from our own, for example. Rhetorical conventions among some Native American tribes, for instance, rely heavily on the establishment of *ethos*. When a reader accustomed to mainstream academic discourse encounters the text of a writer steeped in these rhetorical patterns, she may judge the text to be too heavily narrative and writer-centered, rather than argumentative or expository and reader-centered. When the tutor asks the writer to help her as she tries to understand her own goals and plans for what he has written, she may discover sound reasons for his writing in a manner that seems rambling. Then she can affirm the writer's identification with his cultural tradition as well as communicate her response to the text as a piece of academic discourse.

Reading with an open mind means reading student texts from the same stance with which we approach professional and published literary texts. When we encounter writing like James Joyce's *Ulysses* or Dylan Thomas' "Altarwise by Owlight," for example, our question is, "Why did the author do this, rather than that?" If we were to read these same texts in the way we frequently read student texts, our questions might instead sound something like, "Where did this sentence or paragraph go wrong? Where are the topic sentences?"

Some texts have a place for everything and everything in its place, while others work by surprise. The tutor's key to focus lies in helping writers to articulate their purposes and goals, helping them to become more self-reflexive through offering our services as thoughtful readers and responders to their texts.

Further Reading

Connor, Ulla. 1996. *Contrastive Rhetoric: Cross-cultural Aspects of Second-Language Writing*. New York: Cambridge University Press.

Connor draws on research in ESL/EFL writing to discuss the theory of contrastive rhetoric, which has implications for understanding the link between organization in writing and culture (see Chapter 7, this volume). Using a variety of genres and styles from several first languages, she shows how deeply embedded writing is in culture. Her discussion of the pedagogical implications of this research is valuable for tutors working with native speakers of English as well as for tutors and instructors of ESL/EFL students.

Lawson, Bruce, Susan Sterr Ryan, and W. Ross Winterowd, eds. 1989. *Encountering Student Texts: Interpretive Issues in Reading Student Writing.* Urbana, IL: NCTE.

This collection of essays relates interpretive theory to the practice of reading student writing. Chapters by Janice M. Lauer, "Interpreting Student Writing," and Sharon Crowley, "On Intention in Student Texts," are relevant to understanding how tutors construct a text's organization.

Owen, Derek. 1994. *Resisting Writings (and the Boundaries of Composition).* Dallas, TX: Southern Methodist University Press.

Tutors will be interested in reading Owen's challenge to the teaching of academic discourse as an ethnocentric ideology. He validates a variety of competing rhetorics by quoting from published texts that resist conventional genre definitions. His proposed alternative writing program invites students to practice a variety of styles and genres.

Notes

1. This is a strategy advocated by Gabriele Rico in her text *Writing the Natural Way* (Los Angeles: Tarcher, 1987).
2. Linda S. Flower and John R. Hayes, "A Cognitive Process Theory of Writing," *College Composition and Communication* 32 (1981): 377.
3. Richard Braddock, "The Frequency and Placement of Topic Sentences in Expository Prose," *Research in the Teaching of English* 8 (1974): 287–302.
4. Francis Christensen, "A Generative Rhetoric of the Paragraph." *Notes Toward a New Rhetoric: Six Essays for Teachers.* Reprinted in Francis Christensen (with Bonnijean Christensen), *Notes Toward a New Rhetoric: Nine Essays for Teachers* (New York: Harper and Row, 1978), 77.
5. Christensen, 79.
6. Rich Eden and Ruth Mitchell, "Paragraphing for the Reader," *College Composition and Communication* 37 (1986): 416–30.
7. W. Ross Winterowd, "The Grammar of Coherence," *College English* 31 (1970): 328–35.
8. Frank J. D'Angelo, "The Topic Sentence Revisited," *College Composition and Communication* 37 (1986): 437.
9. Linda Flower, *Problem-Solving Strategies for Writing,* 3d ed. (New York: Harcourt Brace Jovanovich, 1989), ch. 7.
10. Flower and Hayes, 377.
11. Flower and Hayes, 377.
12. Winterowd.
13. For an especially good discussion of cross-cultural conferencing, see Laurel J. Black, *Between Talk and Teaching* (Logan: Utah State University Press, 1998), ch. 4.

Works Cited

Black, L. J. 1998. *Between Talk and Teaching*. Logan: Utah State University Press.

Braddock, R. 1974. "The Frequency and Placement of Topic Sentences in Expository Prose." *Research in the Teaching of English* 8: 287–302.

Christensen, F. 1967. "A Generative Rhetoric of the Paragraph." *Notes Toward a New Rhetoric: Six Essays for Teachers*. Reprinted in F. Christensen (with Bonnijean Christensen), *Notes Toward a New Rhetoric: Nine Essays for Teachers*. New York: Harper and Row, 1978.

D'Angelo, F. 1986. "The Topic Sentence Revisited." *College Composition and Communication* 37: 431–41.

Eden, R., and R. Mitchell. 1986. "Paragraphing for the Reader." *College Composition and Communication* 37: 416–30.

Flower, L. 1989. *Problem-Solving Strategies for Writing*. 3d ed. New York: Harcourt Brace Jovanovich.

Flower, L., and J. Hayes. 1981. "A Cognitive Process Theory of Writing." *College Composition and Communication* 32: 365–87.

Flower, L., D. L. Wallace, L. Norris, and R. E. Burnett, eds. 1994. *Making Thinking Visible: Writing, Collaborative Planning, and Classroom Inquiry*. Urbana, IL: NCTE.

LeFevre, K. 1987. *Invention as a Social Act*. Carbondale: Southern Illinois University Press.

Rico, G. 1983. *Writing the Natural Way*. Los Angeles, CA: Tarcher.

Winterowd, W. R. 1970. "The Grammar of Coherence." *College English* 31: 328–35.

12

Helping Writers to Write Analytically
Ben Rafoth

One of the challenges tutors face in our writing center is assignments that ask students to analyze something. The instructor might ask for an analysis of the way in which two related readings address an issue or controversy or how a period in history was affected by a specific event. College writers seem to recognize that analysis assignments involve thinking about their topic in certain ways—that it doesn't just mean give opinions or write a description—but they often don't know how to go about thinking and writing analytically for the assignment they have. What they lack, as Muriel Harris points out (see Chapter 4), is a sense of how it feels to think and write this particular way, and so they seek help from tutors.

Though helping students to think critically and analytically about their assignments is difficult work for even the most talented tutors, writing centers need to be part of this effort. At the same time, the idea that tutors shoulder this responsibility gives pause. Is "help students to think analytically" in anyone's job description? What does it mean for you to help writers in this way? How does a tutor even begin to help students think analytically about their papers, and what are some complications that can arise from this line of work?

Some Background

Before we consider ways to help writers be more analytical in their writing, we first have to look on writing as a thinking problem, and that necessarily involves entering risky territory. It is easy, though wrong, to make a leap of judgment from a piece of writing to the thinking ability of the writer. The papers students bring to the writing center are snapshots, not movie reels, and they don't begin to represent the full range of a student's ability. Having said that, the purpose of a writing center is to help students become better and more thoughtful writers. One way tutors can encourage this is by asking students to

107

talk with them about their writing. "Our task must involve engaging students in conversation at as many points in both the writing and the reading process as possible," writes Kenneth Bruffee,[1] who believes that talk is essential to thinking. Bruffee goes on to explain:

> The range, complexity, and subtlety of our thought, its power, the practical and conceptual uses we can put it to . . . result in large measure . . . from the degree to which we have been initiated into what Oakeshott calls the potential "skill and partnership" of human conversation in its public and social form.[2]

In other words, says Bruffee, our thoughts are largely a product of the conversations we have with one another. We can sometimes hear these conversation streams replayed in our minds when struggling with a dilemma, like whether to buy a new CD. They are the voices that take us back and forth: "Buy it, you deserve it . . . ," "Save your money, you're going to need it . . . ," "Wait a while and you'll see you don't really want it . . . ," "Oh what the heck. . . ." Bruffee's point is that these subdued voices *are* our thoughts, and they can be enriched by the conversations writers have with tutors, expanding the ways students understand an issue by rendering new intellectual and emotional perspectives or directing their attention to something that has been overlooked.

Helping writers be more analytical in their writing begins with you, the tutor, putting more thought into the way you read and respond. For a writing center to remain committed to the idea of helping writers with ideas, tutors and students must "forge new intellectual partnerships," says David Coogan.[3] The partners must have some knowledge in common for there to be any kind of intellectual relationship, and once this common knowledge is identified you can enter the conversation—not as an all-purpose reader offering generic good advice, but as a specific, individual tutor with particular advice and the occasion to express it. There is no formula for thinking deeper or for the conversation that leads intellectual partners to better writing. As in the game of chess, though, there are plenty of moves that experienced writers use when they have to write analytically, and you can become a more thoughtful responder to student papers by learning some of these moves. They are all around you in the articles and books you are assigned to read in your classes and in the lectures you hear from professors. They appear in newspaper and magazine essays, in debates between experts, and among pundits on television shows like *Meet the Press* and the *Macneil-Lehrer News Hour.* But to recognize them as moves, you have to read or listen with this question in mind: What is the writer or speaker doing, not just saying, to make the points she is making? In other words, you have to assume the writer has a strategy and that it is more than the pure expression of ideas. So, read critically and notice how you are being led, not just from point A to point B, but in a particular way. By enlarging your own awareness of moves, you will become not only a better tutor but a better writer yourself.[4]

For the writers you tutor, you'll need to begin by focusing on the ideas they care about and then stretching them in the give-and-take of conversation—like making taffy, only not as neat.

What to Do

Every tutoring session needs to revolve around a shared purpose, and this is especially true when working with ideas. What is the purpose of the assignment, and what do you both expect to accomplish in the session? Once agreed, you can use the power of conversation to strengthen the ideas in a paper by examining both your own perspective and the writer's, adding layers of complexity, and using borrowed material to enrich the author's own voice.

Examine perspective   An important idea in our postmodern era is that every person reads and writes from a particular set of perspectives in the culture to which they belong. I write as a forty-something English professor and writing center director at a school in rural America, editor of this book, and other perspectives, including many I know more by imagination than direct experience. These perspectives influence how I read and write so that acknowledging where I stand illuminates some of the strengths and limitations of my authority on the subject. It also shows me that what I see comes from my point of view and that changing what I see happens only when I change my perspective. This ultimately leads me to think more deeply and critically about my topic, my audience, and myself. As two writing researchers wrote, "Thinking about your positions makes you conscious of the ways you come to know the way you know."[5] Tutors read and students write from perspectives, too.

My colleague Lea Masiello tells me that in order to find the ripe green beans in her garden, she has to walk around her garden many times, craning her neck, pushing leaves and branches aside. The ripe ones always hide and to find them you have to keep changing your angle of vision. Reading and writing is like this, too, and so two questions for the tutor to begin with are, How might I step into positions that will give me the perspectives I need for understanding or relating to the student and the paper? and How might I understand things differently if I repositioned myself? If you can reflect openly with the writer about these questions, then she may do the same with you and with the way she looks at her own paper. Actually, this is the kind of conversation that must take place when tutors finds themselves deeply at odds with the ideas in a paper; since there cannot be a dialogue with the writer unless there is common ground, the idea of positioning or taking a perspective can provide some common space.[6]

Imagine, for example, that you were reading a paper on a topic about life in another culture and you found the customs rather bizarre. You might wonder what the writer thinks of these customs and how, given your own feelings, you should respond. Should you express the revulsion you feel about reading of a mutilation ritual? What if the writer gives no inkling of her feelings? Will your reaction prejudice her about her own topic? Or will your reaction make her defensive about the culture she is studying? What I'm suggesting is that you have many avenues open to you, just as the writer does. "As an outsider to this culture, I don't understand why they have these customs, which seem bizarre to me," you might say, "but if I were a member of the culture I would probably have a different opinion about them. I'm wondering what different perspectives you might have." The goal is to help the writer think analytically about the paper by seeing the limits of any single position. At the same time that the writer sees how shifting from one perspective to another generates things to say, you, as the tutor, become a more thoughtful reader of the writer's work as well.

Add complexity to the issue   In most academic writing in the humanities and social sciences that calls for analysis of some issue or controversy, a key move is to define and explain problems, not to solve them. Readers want to feel they have learned something from the reading experience or gained an insight; they usually don't expect the writer to hand them a solution because most prefer instead to seek answers on their own in more indirect ways. When I was growing up, my uncle never wanted to follow the directions my dad gave him to get to our house in the country, so each year he took "a quicker route"—twice as long, but he did it his way. When a writer tries to write analytically, you can help by steering the conversation into exploring the complexity of a subject and teasing out the nature of a problem and its effects. Instead of settling the controversy, this will draw it out, but you'll both probably find that this kind of analyzing is more interesting and engaging than zooming toward some pat answer.

Let's assume the writer has written a draft he is ready to revise and that it has a too-simple thesis and scant development. Bearing in mind the previous advice regarding perspective, you might talk a bit about your response to the paper and the lack of engagement you felt as a reader. You can discuss missed opportunities ("As a humanities major, this part really made me curious about . . ."), counterpoints ("Because I grew up in a city, this example makes me think of some counterexamples like . . ."), or point of view ("As somebody who likes to hunt, I understand the gun owners' point of view, but what about other points of view?"). Then work on complicating the thesis statement so that definitions and explanations become central, rather than solutions. Let's see how this might be done with the topic of school violence and its possible relationship to male adolescent depression, something psychologists have been examining recently. Consider this main idea a writer might begin with:

> There are three reasons why male adolescent depression leads to school violence: alienation from peers, distorted sense of reality, and access to weapons.

As the central idea for a paper, this might seem appealing because it's assertive and self-structuring. It says one thing causes another and gives three reasons why. But in fact, it promises so much by way of cause-and-effect relationships that even experts on the subject would shun it. Another approach might look something like this:

> School violence may be related to male adolescent depression, some psychologists argue, while gun control advocates believe that access to weapons is the main factor.

This thesis associates the relationship among depression, violence, and weapons with different perspectives (psychologists, gun control advocates) and it qualifies the claims being made (may be, main factor). It allows for a more complex essay by putting the relationship between these ideas on the table so that the writer can define types of violence that may not be related to depression and explain both the pros and cons of claims. In other words, it tries to put ideas into play rather than nail down the thesis. Once relieved of the burden to defend a hard-to-prove thesis, the conversation you have with the writer can now be about different ways of looking at the issue, the implications that arise from seeing it one way and then another, and the other factors (besides the main one) that might contribute to school violence. In short, once your conversation with the writer has complicated the problem until it feels opened wide up—beyond any hope of a simple solution—the writer is in a better position to examine his idea from multiple perspectives, leaving the reader not with The Solution, which is likely to be inadequate anyway, but with the feeling that a better understanding of the problem has been achieved.

Use outside sources as back-up singers for the author's voice   Aside from showing the professor that the student has read the reading, why do outside sources strengthen a paper? Your writer may need to be reminded why. A professional writer and author of many books about writing, Donald Murray answers the question this way: "Readers are hungry for information. They want images and facts, revealing details and interesting quotations, amazing statistics and insights that make them see, feel and know their world better than they did before the reading."[7] Besides this, I would add, readers enjoy the variety of voices that different sources represent, especially when they are in some form of dialogue with each other. Material integrated from a carefully read article, chapter, or quotation contributes another voice, thereby adding texture to the writing. If you think about it, this is why most singers perform with back-up vocalists, and why we usually prefer listening to a band rather than a soloist. A group contains more interpretations and interactions, making it a more interesting listening experience.

Most writing assignments are related in some way to an assigned reading, which presents an occasion for a different kind of conversation, this time with the ideas of the reading's author. As a tutor, you can help the writer to imagine a dialogue with the reading, like this:

You: The reading says that adolescence is less stressful in traditional cultures than in the West. And you were saying—what was it you said a minute ago?

Writer: Um, I said there probably aren't as many guns in traditional cultures, and that this might be a factor, too.

You: Okay, good. Let's go on. The article says that in the West the emphasis on individualism pushes adolescents to become independent, and you say—how would you respond to that?

Writer: [*Thinks a while*] Well, I'd say that I can see how this is stressful because parents want to control this independence and that leads to conflict.

As you can see from this dialogue, the tutor helps by drawing out ideas. Instead of skimming the reading for anything he can cut and paste from it, the writer can now follow the thread of an idea with the tutor's help, weaving it between the article and his own thoughts. This kind of dialogue keeps the writer engaged with the reading instead of just plucking quotable quotes from it. At some point you may have to point out that superficial writing tends to be dotted with drop-in quotes and references wherever they'll fit (usually the end of paragraphs). It's a little like name dropping ("As the great Shakespeare once said . . ."). In-depth, thoughtful writing is more likely to integrate quotes so tightly that if you tried to remove them, you would almost have to rewrite the entire paragraph. To help writers appreciate how it works, keep an example handy and invite them to remove the quotation and notice how the paragraph falls apart. I tried to illustrate this type of integration with the Donald Murray quote in the first paragraph in this section. I used Murray's words first to answer a question ("Why do outside sources") and then later to make a related point I wanted to include ("Besides this").

Complicating Matters

I have tried to show a few ways you can use conversation to help writers think analytically about their papers. As I was writing this chapter, though, I kept imagining *yes-buts*. Let me share a couple of them with you now.

How much subject-area knowledge must you have before being able to help a writer write analytically? Can you be effective without *any* subject-area knowledge, relying only on common sense? While people who collaborate in the workplace tend to be from the same area or department, writing center tutors tend to work with students on most any assignment in any subject (although some writing centers do have policies on this matter). This same dilemma faces most composition instructors, whose classes are comprised of students from many different majors, raising again the question of just how discipline-specific writing instruction should be at the college level. There is no easy answer to this, and I think you have to rely on your good judgment and training to know when you're in over your head. With some topics, that point may come quickly, and you should discuss your limitations with the writer (see Chapter 13).

A second complication arises from the fact that helping writers to think analytically does not come easily, and not all tutors in a writing center may be comfortable with the idea of helping students in a way that appears to challenge the ideas a writer is trying to convey. They may agree with a tutor in the writing center where I work who once said he believed that students want tutors who will be supportive of their efforts, not tutors who will complicate them.

But a supportive tutor is not just a cheerleader—he's a constructive critic as well. Ideas, arguments, and values are what writing is about, and students who come to a writing center need a real audience. If the writer's paper seems to lack any kind of analysis or deeper thought, who better to hear it from than a peer? The important thing is how this message is delivered and how supported the writer feels in making the necessary changes. Sometimes writers don't want to change what they've written simply because it took them so long to write it. This is even more reason for you to respond genuinely to the work that students do, because if a student has worked very hard yet produced something that looks as though it was dashed off in twenty minutes, then something is very wrong. For such a writer, the writing center must now become a site of productive tension, a place where thinking and writing analytically begin to create the conflicts that promote growth. It is not the last place of learning for the writer, but it may be the beginning.

Further Reading

Dinitz, Sue, Jean Kiedaisch, and William Mierse. 1997. "Tutor Positioning in Group Sessions." *Writing Lab Newsletter* 21 (5): 11, 14.

This article gives tutors some insights into the authoritative and nonauthoritative roles they play when meeting with writers and how the writers perceive these roles. After studying videotapes of actual tutoring sessions, the authors were surprised by the limitations of roles they thought would be effective and the effectiveness of roles they thought would be quite limited. This study is interesting for what it reveals about the perspective that tutors bring to the session.

Flynn, Thomas, and Mary King. 1993. *Dynamics of the Writing Conference.* Urbana, IL: NCTE.

Although this collection of essays is geared more for graduate students and researchers than for undergraduates, it is still recommended reading for anyone interested in investigating relationships between critical thinking and writing conferences. The first chapter, "Promoting Higher Order Thinking Skills in Writing Conferences," is especially helpful.

Kuriloff, Peshe C. 1996. "What Discourses Have in Common: Teaching the Transaction Between Writer and Reader." *College Composition and Communication* 47 (4): 485–501.

Written by the director of a writing-across-the-curriculum program, this article addresses a controversy mentioned in this chapter concerning just how discipline-specific writing instruction needs to be at the college level. Do people in one field write all that differently from those in another, or is there common ground that tutors can become familiar with? This article offers some insights.

Notes

1. Kenneth Bruffee, "Collaborative Learning and the 'Conversation of Mankind,'" *College English* 46 (7) (1984): 642.

2. Bruffee, 640.

3. David Coogan, "E-mail 'Tutoring' as Collaborative Writing," in *Wiring the Center,* ed. Eric H. Hobson (Logan: Utah State University Press, 1998), 30.

4. Research indicates that expert tutors are self-aware; they reflect on themselves as tutors and writers. See Bennett A. Rafoth and Erin K. Murphy, "Expertise in Tutor- ing," *Maryland English Journal* 29 (1) (Fall 1994): 1–9.

5. Elizabeth Chiseri-Strater and Bonnie Stone Sunstein, *FieldWorking* (Upper Saddle River, NJ: Blair Press of Prentice Hall, 1997), 59.

6. While I believe it is important for students to explore the various perspectives they might take, the fact remains that instructors sometimes make it difficult to do this when they make assignments that shoehorn them into choosing from a very limited set of perspectives. The assignment might restrict writers by requiring them to argue for or against one side or the other. Or the restriction might be more subtle, as when an assignment assumes certain values or backgrounds that the students may in fact not share with the instructor. In these cases, I recommend that you continue to explore different perspectives in the tutoring session and then urge the writer to meet with the instructor to discuss why she wants to take a somewhat different approach than what the assignment calls for. At some point, you might wish to read what Mar- ilyn Cooper has to say on the problem of assignments that limit the writer's set of positions (also see Chapter 10, this volume).

7. Donald Murray, *The Craft of Revision,* 2d ed. (New York: Harcourt Brace, 1995), 74.

Works Cited

Bruffee, K. 1984. "Collaborative Learning and the 'Conversation of Mankind,'" *Col- lege English* 46 (7): 635–52.

Chiseri-Strater, E., and B. S. Sunstein. 1997. *FieldWorking.* Upper Saddle River, NJ: Blair Press of Prentice Hall.

Coogan, D. 1998. "E-mail 'Tutoring' as Collaborative Writing." In *Wiring the Center,* ed. E. H. Hobson, 25–43. Logan: Utah State University Press.

Cooper, M. 1994. "Really Useful Knowledge: A Cultural Studies Agenda for Writing Centers." *Writing Center Journal* 14 (2): 97–111.

Harris, M. 1995. "Talking in the Middle: Why Writers Need Writing Tutors." *College English* 57 (1): 27–42.

Murray, D. 1995. *The Craft of Revision.* 2d ed. New York: Harcourt Brace.

Rafoth, B. A., and E. K. Murphy. 1994. "Expertise in Tutoring." *Maryland English Journal* 29 (1) (Fall): 1–9.

13

Tutoring in Unfamiliar Subjects

Alexis Greiner

Writing centers are expected to help students with papers on topics ranging from bouillabaisse to Brazil nuts. While it may seem advantageous to everyone if the writing center staff included someone from every major, this is not realistic or even necessarily desirable. The fact is, writing center consultants, like most composition instructors, help students from all majors and disciplines learn to write. This is true at Rollins College, where I worked as a writing center tutor, and at most writing centers.

Before going any further, I believe it is important to distinguish between a *writing center consultant*, the term used at Rollins and the one I will use in this chapter, and an *academic tutor*. At Rollins, we consider a *tutor* to be someone who helps a student with subject matter, while a *writing center consultant* does not share this goal. Consultants help by provoking thought through conversation, posing questions, and engaging writers in the work of writing. A consultant also helps by urging the student to write because the act of writing is itself a valuable way for writers to discover what they do and do not know about their topic and to figure out what they want to say in their papers. If you are reading this book, you are probably what we at Rollins call a consultant.

How can a consultant majoring in a field such as communication help a student who is writing a paper on a topic like finitely quantifiable abstractions in calculus? At some point, every consultant must recognize when the knowledge gap is too wide and the writer needs to be referred back to the professor for help. The knowledge gap can be a problem even when the consultant and writer are in the same field. Extreme cases are the exception, however, and most of the time tutors can be helpful to writers even when they do not share the same background knowledge on a topic.

Rollins is a liberal arts school where cross-disciplinary writing is an important aspect of the curriculum. By placing our focus more on writing aspects than on the content or subject matter, we are able to use a similar approach with most papers. This makes it possible to fulfill our mission of helping writers across the broad spectrum of the curriculum.

Some Background

Most literature on writing and writing center theory discusses feedback and conversation, the crux of consulting on a paper you know little about. Peter Elbow details two kinds of feedback: criterion-based and reader-based. The first helps the writer to assess content, thesis, organization, effectiveness of language, and diction. Student writers are most accustomed to criterion-based feedback. Reader-based feedback, on the other hand, leaves the technical stuff behind while the reader expresses the *experience* he gains from reading. Both are useful, but they are applicable in different ways, and at different stages.

Reader-based feedback is a great way to approach unfamiliar matters because it says to the reader, "Look, this is not my field, but your tone and flow reached me through the difficult vocabulary." Or, "The vocabulary you use is specific and difficult, and your writing needs to be super clear to compensate. I feel confused." In such circumstances it is useful to ask clients to assume a reader's role and try to distance themselves from their own writing—so that they can view the paper from a perspective different from their own. This, as Donald Murray says, is in the spirit of teaching students to teach themselves.

What to Do

In the Rollins writing center, like most writing centers, consultants approach each paper in a top-down manner, meaning that we move from a global to a local assessment (see Chapters 1 and 16). Here is a sample from a consultation with a client I'll call Ann. First of all, notice how Ann responds to my question about the assignment.

Meeting and Assignment

Me: OK, then, let's get started. What is the assignment?

Ann: Well, I wrote a paper on quantum physics and the nature of the protein RNA synthetase and then connected the ideas.

Instead of describing the assignment, which would require her to take her instructor's point of view, Ann tells me what she wrote her paper on. But the two may or may not match, and an experienced consultant knows that now is a good time for a reality check. Ask the client to read the assignment aloud, or at least to consider how her paper does what the assignment asks. (In this example, it turns out that Ann's paper has followed the assignment.) Next, look for key points.

Review Drafting and Pick Out One or Two Key Points

Me: OK. What have you done so far?

Ann: I have written two drafts and now I am trying to get it into a clearer shape to turn in.

Me: Alright, could you, in a sentence maybe, tell me what the connection is that you have found between the ideas?

Ann: I'll try. During cell reproduction there is an interaction between proteins that is affected by laws of quantum physics. I think that is the key to the whole thing.

Me: It sounds like *affected* is a key term. Would you agree? [*Ann agrees*] What exactly do you mean by *affected*? I ask because its meaning might be the focus of your paper.

Ann: Well, some of the protein behavior is limited, and some of it is made possible by these laws. And yes, I think that is the focus.

Me: You seem to have a clear grasp on the basics of your idea. Which is a good thing, because it's Greek to me! Let me ask you something else before I read it. Are you comfortable with the organization of your ideas?

Notice how the tutor (me) tries to pick up on things the writer says to help focus attention on what seem like key points. Also, notice how the tutor depends on Ann to confirm what the tutor thinks Ann is getting at. Let's continue.

Read with a Focus

Ann: Yeah, pretty much. I am more used to writing straightforward lab reports, but this is a little different. I wrote it as an essay for a journal, so I modified the structure to include an abstract and then all the rest of it is like a big discussion of the results.

Me: Good. I'll go ahead and read through it now, and I'll focus on the clarity of *affected* and the other things you've told me, and we'll work from there, OK?

Ann: Sounds good.

All consulting is about discovery through conversation, and this situation is no different. If consultants do not know the subject matter, they can use their own curiosity to draw ideas out of the client. By asking the writer to explain what he knows and to view the paper from a distance, the consultant can help the client use his own knowledge to greater advantage in the writing process.

In my experience and those of other consultants at Rollins, the most commonly noted problem is that the work needs better clarity, usually at the paragraph and sentence level, through improved style and diction. If I notice this in Ann's paper, I do not say it immediately. First I engage her in conversation about what she has written.

Test Out Ideas

Me: Ann, I took this sentence here to be your thesis.

Ann: Good—that was my intention.

Me: And then I thought that you used the following paragraphs to support your thesis. Real quickly, I'd like to go through each paragraph and tell you what I got from it in a nutshell. Again, this is not my area, so if I miss something I want you to tell me.

Then,

Ask Thought-Provoking Questions and Build on the Client's Response

Me: This is hard for me to understand. It seems like you are putting forth a formula and then you explain why it works in those reactions. Is that right?

Ann: Close, but not really. I was trying to illustrate a flaw in a fairly well-known theorem as it applies to intercellular interactions.

Me: Ahh. OK, you could make that really clearer to me by introducing the flaw—"A well-known theorem that has held true in some cases does not in this one . . . "—and so on.

Ann: Oh yeah. That's a good idea.

Me: Go ahead and write, if you want. I'll wait.

I try to establish a pattern that adheres closely to the writer's text and work on that rather than getting into a discussion about general principles of organization, which may not apply in this case (see Chapter 11).

There are many ways to make the consultation valuable by relying on your skills at conversation. Be confident in your ability to provide feedback the writer can use. Remember, too, that the client knows that you are not in her field and you can remind her to take this into account when hearing your feedback. If you are still unsure about what to say to the writer or how to be helpful, be frank about your doubts and let the writer tell you what kind of feedback she feels would be most productive—asking thought-provoking questions, perhaps, or working on specific aspects that may be subject-independent or quasi-independent, like organization, tone, diction, sentence structure, and flow. Be confident of your ability to reach a mutual understanding with the writer.

Complicating Matters

Probably the most important thing to be concerned about when working with a client on an unfamiliar topic is to be sure that she understands the limits of your background knowledge and to be sure that you are both in agreement on how best to approach the paper. By explaining your limitations, you ensure that the client is informed about what she can expect from her visit to the writing center, and by agreeing on the approach you ensure a good chance for bringing what you have to offer as close as possible to what she needs.

When reading a text in an unfamiliar subject, it is easy to feel put off by the language and even the tone of the work. It may sound jargon-filled and be frustrating to read and follow. While these responses are natural, it is important to trust the writer's instincts and not try to change the writing to reflect your sense of how an essay should sound. This is important because your client probably has a better sense of the writing in her discipline than you do, yet she may not yet fully trust her own instincts and might yield to your advice thinking you are a writing expert. In short, if you cannot articulate a reason for why you think something should be changed, leave it alone, and trust the client's ear over your own about how the paper sounds. (See Chapter 3.)

Finally, as a way of learning about writing standards in different disciplines, I recommend inviting faculty from those disciplines to writing center staff meetings, especially if they tend to refer their students to the writing center a lot. Keeping a diverse staff of tutors helps, too. In the end, though, it all comes down to you and the student, maybe even someone with a paper on finitely quantifiable abstractions. Try to understand the paper as best you can, be frank about your limitations, and build on ideas the writer brings up in conversation.

Further Reading

Blair, Catherine Pastore. 1988. "Only One of the Voices: Dialogic Writing Across the Curriculum." *College English* 50 (April): 383–89.

If your school has a writing-across-the-curriculum (WAC) program, this article may be of interest. Many supporters of WAC suggest that each academic discipline has its own way of using language, which can be understood only in its own disciplinary context. Tutors will be interested in Blair's argument that the discipline of English knows only its own way of using language, not all the others, and does not provide an all-purpose academic discourse. So, Blair says, there is no reason for all writing instruction to be taught by the English department faculty. A WAC program should be taught instead by faculty from all disciplines. One possible implication of Blair's article is that tutors can at best know only the discourse of their own disciplines—a different perspective than the one I offer in this chapter.

Gillespie, Paula, and Neal Lerner, eds. 2003. *The Allyn and Bacon Guide to Peer Tutoring*. 2d ed. New York: Longman.

Chapter 13 of this book offers a good selection of scenarios for discussion with your director or other tutors. Other chapters in this book cover expectations about tutoring, effective practices, and writing center research.

Kennedy, Mary Lynch, William J. Kennedy, and Hadley M. Smith. 2003. *Writing in the Disciplines*. 5th ed. Upper Saddle River, NJ: Prentice Hall.

This is one of a number of books that deals with the different standards and conventions for writing in the sciences, humanities, and social sciences. Another is *The Harcourt Brace Guide to Writing in the Disciplines* by Patrick Bizzaro and Robert W. Jones (1997). Though not a substitute for the knowledge about writing that someone in the field has, books like this are a good reference to keep on the shelf in your writing center.

Works Cited

Elbow, P. 1998. *Writing with Power.* 2d ed. New York: Oxford University Press.

Murray, D. 1985. *A Writer Teaches Writing.* 2d ed. Boston: Houghton Mifflin.

14

Developing Genre Discourse

Graduate Student Writing

Carol Ellis

Graduate student writing is high stakes. From here to a career. Schooled in theories and methodologies, the writer feels compelled to hit it out of the park, but ends up searching for a place just to enter the conversation. On quiet days the staff—we call them neither tutors nor consultants but instructors—and I sit around and talk, reenacting Roland Barthes' "pleasure of the text."[1] There is laughter. At least once a day we laugh because laughter lightens the seriousness and creates community in a commuter graduate school of two thousand students where loneliness is part of the price of learning. We create necessary community through talking. We are open twelve months of the year, ready to discover the thesis statement cleverly buried on page ten.

The instructors in this graduate writing center use reader response, blatant curiosity, and questioning to show that writing itself is a genre and thus not obvious, not something arbitrary: it has to be worked up. They instruct writing workshops of their own designs. They walk the talk. The staff of the writing center writes and reads session proposals for conferences, essays for a variety of graduate courses, theses, and dissertations. As Derridian difference is written into being, they become comfortable with the diversity of styles, genders, and cultures that descend into our basement. Beside tutoring appointments, every summer there is a five-week writing workshop on writing articles for professional journals in the disciplines, a continuous creative writing workshop, and a weekly conversation with someone who is finally ready to write a dissertation after four years of research. We are impressed by the responsibility we handle.

"I'm on the go," my mother used to say when she was very busy. "I'm running around like a madwoman." Although I am not mad, writing center directors often have the desire to be so as a way of taking a short vacation. There is no escaping the issue of identity in university culture, though. Who is a writing

121

center director? When does a graduate student become a graduate instructor in the writing center? What do we do down there in the basement? I learn the immense difference between staff and faculty as they are perceived and paid. As a director of the graduate writing center, I am staff, immediately less respected by the institution. I have the experience of being in graduate school every day as a mentor, adviser, and teacher to graduate students whom I consider my colleagues. We are all here because we value academic culture and discourse. The work we do paves a road that winds through dissertations, groups of international students, workshops, and individual appointments that are supposed to last for an hour and be limited to one appointment per week per client, although we regularly break the rules we did not create.

Some Background

For the small but growing number of graduate writing centers in the United States, writers think writing does all things at once, which is one reason it is difficult to do well, and so we create our theory on the go. We invent definitions and hone the genre of graduate student discourse. Graduate students struggle with the definition of writing for the graduate classroom, a definition swinging between respect for tradition and desire for insurrection. This is our backdrop.

> They look at each other across a small table where they sit in two separate chairs. There is no wine, no lit candles, no flowers one of them brought to the other. Papers and books serve as a tablecloth. They met only moments before when one stood in the doorway and held white pages outstretched to the other, who looked up and smiled. The invitation is extended to come in and sit down. They look down at the paper that experienced the risk of writing and will now experience the risk of rewriting. Sunlight comes through the windows and washes over the plants. This is a safe room to talk about words as they move from desire to consummation then back to desire in the time a sentence happens. They read a sentence. One says the words aloud, the other listens. Together they think of change. One suggests, the other waves a pen through the air until it lands on the page. They glance at each other again and continue. They are in graduate school, swinging on a tire hung from a tree limb. They define writing as they untangle text. They are wealthy with dreams, and only there do they touch, each dreaming of knowing more than anyone knows. Voices come from other rooms built by conversations that curve around what needs to be written and what wants to be written. They write in the direction they want their lives to determine; some pages might be published or presented at conferences, other pages churned into diplomas. The power of pages terrifies.

One of the tasks of the tutor who works with graduate students is to break through the caution, the fear of not meeting discipline-specific standards, before the majesty of invention is tossed aside and the student becomes a master of repeating the good work that has already occurred (see Chapter 10). As they sit together and talk, how does the instructor express compromise without compromising the writer? Academia determines the text and what can be done with it as it asks to be written and rewritten by writers who often become too cautious to do the work. The risk of writing is the risk inherent in any art; self-expression demands a self, and the graduate student is a self in transition, a self learning to learn. If this self guesses incorrectly, the world appears to crash and burn, so intense is the desire to learn the craft without destroying the art. What appears to be an innocent conversation between student and instructor is not innocent at all. They are creating a world in which the intellect discovers and recovers its texts. At this moment in the writing center, together they own the territory of writing for graduate school.

Still, who owns graduate student writing? Aristotle? A memory? Who wrote it? The writer in a burst of fearless intellectual vitality? The discipline whose restrictions are its definitions? The methodology? The reader in the writing center? Perhaps the text is owned by the writer's home language—not English then, but English now (see Chapter 6). Who owns the dissertation? Part of being a writing center director is listening to conversations while appearing to be mesmerized by the bulletin board in the hall outside of our main office. Who owns the conversation? What is the methodology of a graduate writing center whose synapses mutate with every new piece of student writing? Good questions, too many of them, but good ones.

What We Do

Well, alright. The client sits at the table with a quantitative study in political science on a nation that the instructor, a specialist in Renaissance England, didn't know existed until now. "What are you working on today?" she asks. The answer sends her into a whirlwind of private panicky thoughts (in parentheses): (Forty-five more minutes—and I'm outta here.) "How interesting," the instructor chimes after hearing a five-hundred-word themed response. (What more could he have to say in the paper?) Looking at the pages splayed on the table, she offers, "I can see you've been working hard." (Life's a bitch and then you have to write.) "What is your thesis?" (Whatever it is I won't understand it. I think I hate you. I know I hate political science and I also know that all numbers can be manipulated into false truths. I hate numbers.) "Excellent idea! We should make it more prominent. With your thesis on page twenty, the reader might have trouble seeing where your essay enters the conversation on this issue." (Whatever it is. Why am I nodding my head so enthusiastically?)

"The questions you imply are intriguing. Tell me about your methodology." (I'm holding my breath. Breathe. I'm not taking all those yoga classes to forget how to breathe my way into *prana*, nor do I understand a word—wait I understood that word—of what this student is talking about, although I am listening intently; in fact, I have begun to stare either at the student or at the essay. My left leg is shaking; I want to run from the room. Yet the essay appears to be improving and the student is smiling.) "Yes, we do have the book on APA citations. Over there. No, the big one." (What am I, a walking handbook? Look it up yourself.) "OK. Here is an example of what you are looking for. Take a look." (I do MLA, after all, and somehow that feels more rarefied, less commercial, although it appears to change every year.) "Now how are you going to end what you have been saying? Whose 'excellent perceptions' (still hidden) are best for concluding?" (What is your conclusion? Yes, you need a conclusion. You know you need a conclusion.) "How would you conclude? Let's play around with some possibilities." (Have you heard of spell check? Or is this how your discipline spells these words?) "So is what we're doing here helpful to you, you think?" (Or doesn't it matter, because you'll get a job and I'll be outside begging on the streets.)

"What other areas give you trouble in your writing? Ah, how interesting, read it aloud." (My life troubles me.) "Good, you caught that; better fix it now so you remember." (I don't know what you caught, but as long as you do, that's what matters. I wonder if my writing is terrible. I'm hungry. All we have around this place is hard candy, black coffee, bottled water, and one bottle of beer.) "Sounds much better." (You give good ownership.) "You're welcome. Another appointment with me? Sure." As quickly as this appointment leaves, another arrives. I hear the conversation begin in another room. The client is preparing a session proposal for a national conference. The proposal revolves around an issue involving the English Renaissance. I hear, "Oh. How interesting." I silently commend the instructor, who I know is also involved in creating a proposal for the very same conference. They could create a panel together. They could. Thinking it is a brilliant idea, I brazenly interrupt their session to call the instructor out of the room and make my suggestion. The instructor looks at me, says "I don't think so," and disappears back into the room, only to give a further, "but thank you." We are nothing if not polite. Out of this process of attention, doubt, questioning, and self-questioning, dialogue with self and other, come the tasks of writing. It's what we do.

What to do when the paper is a dissertation that emerges in yet another conversation. The ongoing dissertation workshop attracts the largest population during the fall semester. Students become convinced they know nothing of their topic and return to research; or they discover that not everyone is up to the task of chairing a dissertation, as they try, but fail, to get a straight answer from their committee chair, or even any answer at all; or they learn what it means to have a long conversation about the most obscure, creative topic they can think up and tell a long story in a dark room late at night when the raven squawks "Nevermore." Nevertheless, they decide to investigate topics, ranging from what is written in the margins of Renaissance manuals to cocaine use among the homeless as a function of cocaine use at the University of California, Los Angeles. By that time in the semester, it isn't so hard to find volunteers.

We sit in a room together once a week and talk about their dissertations. The population is both consistent and variable. We sit in a room with two windows. We sit around a large, oval seminar table. Each meeting of the workshop begins with the same questions: what you are working on? what made you choose that topic? how is your topic consistent with the direction of your discipline? where do you want to enter the conversation that your discipline assumes it is having now? Each student at the table tells the topic or the lack of a topic, and the graduate student instructor who works with me and is writing her own dissertation on girl culture as expressed through the history of the Camp Fire Girls, attempts to get an optimistic conversation happening.

Instructor: What is your dissertation topic?

Student: I don't know. I can't think anymore. I'm exhausted, and now I have to write a book.

Instructor: It's not a book, it's a dissertation.

Student: What's the difference?

Instructor: A dissertation is what you are writing and a book is what you are not writing. They are two different genres. A book is what gets published, hideously difficult to do in an unhappy economy, so until then you deal in manuscript genres and tenure is a sweet dream. A dissertation is the first draft of a book. A dissertation suffers from first thoughts. You have only begun to write.

Student: Whatever. I have nothing to write about and never will. I have nothing to say. What was wrong with me, thinking someone like me could get a Ph.D.

Instructor: You can get a Ph.D. Just write your dissertation.

Student: How?

Instructor: What fascinates you? What passions tremor the ground you walk on? What are you very interested in? What do you think about? Where do you want to enter the conversations in your discipline?

Student: That's the trouble. I'm not having any conversations. I've lost the ability to think.

Instructor: What questions are you asking? What do you notice when it's time to notice? Notice yourself.

Student: Play.

Instructor: What?

Student: Play. I notice play.

This student went on to complete a dissertation about play as holy, powerful action in the role of the ministry. Really. We teach students to honor their work as academic research and to honor themselves by acknowledging their identities as academic researchers. The ideas about play as potent action and not merely idle engagement and the readings touching upon play were all written down in a researcher's notebook, our name for the journal that every student keeps, from the end of course work to the completion of her dissertation. It helps the writer to develop ideas through thinking, writing, and reading—and to assert the importance of the writer-researcher in the transition from graduate student to graduate degree.[2]

My own experiences in graduate school similarly reflect the journey of revision and reinvention. The writer is the written. The written is the writer. You choose. I wrote my dissertation on a white male American poet who enchanted me with his language, and while enchantment is good, someone ought to have mentioned to me that the academic job market had its fill of white male poets, and with each word I was writing myself away from being hired. A dissertation is transformative, as is all writing for learning, so that when the velvet hood is raised, it comes down on a changed individual. The graduate student becomes the dissertation. For a period of time in my life, I became this particular white male poet; much to my own detriment, I was James Wright.[3]

When a student begins to understand how writing improves, it improves even more when she understands how it interacts with discipline-specific intention. For example, language interacts with history, affecting how we think about an occasion or event. Whose words does the historian listen to? Whose words are lost forever? Over time, writing creates disciplines and the scholars who inhabit them. I wanted to learn all I could about poetry when I was a graduate student in English at the University of Iowa. I did. Then I had to reinvent myself as a writing theorist because the job market continues to bloom in areas of basic writing, composition, and writing pedagogy. My reinvention occurred through using language to understand what I had been doing all along—writing. Personal reinvention and textual revision mirror each other. Getting the entire university community to use writing for learning is the goal of every writing center director and staff (see Chapter 10).

Contemplating Matters

How does thought evolve as it becomes even more educated and how does the student experience this evolution? Thought evolves through conversation, but you have to know there is one going on. At first, students experience the conversation as noise, like the spaces between radio channels. Eventually, they find a conversation and try to break into it with a flourish of trumpets. By the time they are ready to graduate, they are lucky if they have heard a lull and played a few bars. Yet the not-entirely-learned academic game can give graduate student writing an edge. Creative nonfiction, for example, can encourage the writer's identification with the text to be revealed, opening the canon further into intriguing possibilities of style and thought expressed by whoever owns the text (see Chapter 9). Is there a text in this text? If so, what does it say? To paraphrase Stanley Fish,[4] is there a writer in this text, and which of the many cultures of the writer is writing this piece that we look at, sitting here together for an hour or so? A good conversation will answer the questions.

To enter the conversation is to understand the conversation, to define it, to know the language. While many graduate students think ABD means All But Dead, it actually means they are moments away from entering the conversation with their dissertation. It is the tutor's job to remind the graduate students that they really are intrigued by, and want to write about, their topics, and that a mind learning through writing can be ecstasy. To be ABD is to be invited to open a door to the academic discipline that turns and looks at you. You return the gaze with the help of the writing center tutor who tells you to look and look again, and you do because suddenly someone is writing and it is you. From here to a career. That's what we do; we connect the writer to the text and commit the text to academia.

Further Reading

Bishop, Wendy. 1997. *Teaching Lives*. Logan: Utah State University Press.

A collection of some of Wendy's best pieces, this book is a celebration of teaching and the teaching life. Her emphasis on creative freedom as pedagogy and creative nonfiction as an aesthetic stance extends the discussion of ownership and voice.

Bloom, Lynn Z. 1998. *Composition Studies as Creative Art*. Logan: Utah State University Press.

An optimistic discussion of academic culture that asserts change and creativity in teaching, writing, scholarship, and administration, all in an attempt to loosen the grip of archaic and repressive academic systems on the many new voices and ideas that tutors and clients bring to classrooms and writing centers.

Tomkins, Jane. 1996. *A Life in School: What the Teacher Learned*. Reading, MA: Perseus.

Tomkins continues the discussion about pedagogy and discourse with self-ethnography. Teaching is learning. What do you still need to learn? Learn it. Then move on and learn something else. Writing is a process because life is a process. Engage the process. You are continuous.

Notes

1. "Thus the Biblical myth is reversed, the confusion of tongues is no longer a punishment, the subject gains access to bliss by the cohabitation of languages *working side by side*: the text of pleasure is a sanctioned Babel." From Roland Barthes, *The Pleasure of the Text* (New York: Hill and Wang, 1975), 3–4.

2. Based on the dissertation work of Jennifer Helgren Hillman, forthcoming: *"A Beautiful and Useful Womanhood": The Camp Fire Girls and Twentieth-Century Girls'*

Culture in America. Jennifer worked with me on our dissertation workshops while writing her own dissertation, lived to tell about it, and finished.

3. James Wright, *Above the River: The Complete Poems* (New York: Farrar, Straus, & Giroux and University Press of New England, 1990).

4. Stanley Fish, *Is There a Text in This Class?* (Cambridge, MA: Harvard, 1982).

Works Cited

Barthes, R. 1975. *The Pleasure of the Text.* Trans. by Richard Miller. New York: Hill and Wang.

Fish, S. 1982. *Is There a Text in This Class?* Cambridge, MA: Harvard.

Wright, J. 1990. *Above the River: The Complete Poems.* New York: Farrar, Straus & Giroux and University Press of New England.

15

Protocols and Process in Online Tutoring

George Cooper, Kara Bui, and Linda Riker

Online writing technology has slowly begun to change the way some writing centers work, enabling students to submit drafts of essays or rough outlines to a writing center tutor via the campus computer network. The most advanced online operations use email attachments, which transmit files directly from a word processing program but can involve compatibility problems. Other online systems rely exclusively on email, which is user-friendly but not very convenient for sending formatted files. In either case, instead of having to visit the writing center, students can get help with their papers from their residence hall or their hometown, eliminating the need to make a trip to the writing center. But does online tutoring change the nature of teaching and learning that has made writing centers so successful? What are some things tutors must know about online tutoring, and how can they make it effective?

Some Background

Collaborative, face-to-face communication has become a hallmark of the work that peer tutors do in campus writing centers. In her essay "Collaboration, Control, and the Idea of a Writing Center," Andrea Lunsford writes about collaboration and how important it is for students to take control of the tutoring situation. She describes a writing center as a place where "knowledge [is] always contextually bound . . . always constructed" and where, in Hanna Arendt's words, "for excellence, the presence of others is required."[1] In *The Practical Tutor,* Emily Meyer and Louise Smith address a similar issue in their chapter "Engaging in Dialogue." They emphasize that conversation is the precursor to development of ideas on paper. Conversation is a familiar aspect of our oral world, and it is necessary for the writer's transition into the written world. In an effort to cultivate the dialogue of conversations, some researchers emphasize the use of open-ended questions. So important is conversation that Meyer and Smith include a section entitled "Pace and Tone of Questions," pinpointing the prominent role that dialogue assumes in their notion of good tutoring.

Online tutoring stretches and stresses the viability of these good principles. One could argue that sending a paper online to a tutor can be similar to dropping off dry cleaning—leave your paper at the center on Monday and pick it up on Tuesday with all errors marked and corrected—a practice resisted in most writing centers. We train our tutors in collaborative learning and see ourselves as facilitators of knowledge, not dictators of it. Not surprisingly, our tutors question whether the success of face-to-face tutoring can be transferred to online tutoring. "How do we engage the student in dialogue when there is really only one of us present at a time?" they ask. "What kinds of questions should we ask to get the writer's attention?" "How can I tell whether the student understands my comments?"

Though principles of face-to-face tutoring do not transfer completely to online tutoring, we can still retain a sense of collaboration and humanity in the online forum. There are online strategies for establishing a relationship between the tutor and writer, for empowering writers to share in their own revision, and for dealing with specifics of grammar and mechanics—all done by relying on collaborative techniques and leading to a facilitated knowledge between tutor and client. As Barbara Monroe writes in "The Look and Feel of the OWL Conference," "Owl [online writing lab], then, is not just an online tutorial service, but a site where meaning and value are shared, contested and negotiated, a site that provokes and promotes new literate practices, both online and in print."[2] Embracing these principles does not solve all problems—and face-to-face tutoring has problems too—but it does result in a shared learning experience. Moreover, we have found that students using our OWL (online writing and learning) service not only benefit from the feedback but even utilize the directed responses more freely, independently, and self-confidently than they sometimes do in face-to-face tutoring. In the following section, we offer some advice, based on an actual online submission and response, for how to make the benefits of online tutoring a reality.

What to Do

Setting the Right Tone in Introductory Remarks

The writer's first encounter with an online tutor sets the tone for everything that follows. If the tutor's opening remarks are friendly and informal—as they are in the example with its friendly greeting, contractions, and helpful explanations—the writer will read the tutor's comments as gentle and constructive.

Hi Morton,

I'm Lisa, the OWL tutor who'll be reading your paper. I've read through your questions and will make some notes within your paper about the intro, conclusion, overall structure of your paper and grammar. I'll also try to include major questions I have, as a reader, as I read, so you can get an idea of how an average reader might react. Look for my notes within the body of your paper, set off by asterisks, like this****.

But if the comments are businesslike or formal ("Morton, I read your paper and will make some comments about your introduction"), the writer may hear a cold and scolding voice, even if the tutor intended otherwise. Written feedback works this way, and keeping the tone lighthearted and friendly is more than a nicety. It is what stands in place of a smile, eye contact, and pleasant voice.

Muriel Harris writes of the importance of this phase of the tutoring session as "getting acquainted time." It is where tutors learn "students' interests and skills, information useful in helping students locate potential subjects for writing."[3] This period of time includes some social and some academic or intellectual engagements. A tutor might begin with small talk about the weather or a detail about the person's dress that sparks conversation. Such small talk is a necessary first step in establishing trust, and the conversation soon moves toward the student's paper and what kind of help the writer is seeking. The complete process is one which Harris describes as including "getting acquainted time," "diagnostic time," "instructional time," and "evaluation time."[4]

Online writing and learning (OWL) environments allow for some of the same processes. Our OWL at the University of Michigan asks students who are submitting papers to include basic facts like their name, year of enrollment, and course, but it also asks students to describe the assignment and to tell what kind of help they want. This provides the same foundation of information needed in any tutoring session.

When the writer has to type in the assignment and the nature of his writing problem, he has more time to think about what to say, hopefully avoiding "Oh, just check the grammar," a request students often make when they walk into the writing center and can't think quickly enough, or don't know how to ask for help in a more specific way. Some online writing centers offer students a prioritized checklist of potential problem areas (transitions, use of details, punctuation, and so on) and ask them to describe the help they seek in each particular area. In this way, the student takes the initiative to set the agenda.

Although online comments do tend to get to the point much quicker than face-to-face tutoring, it is important to remember that the online tutor still needs to establish a relationship. By the same token, the writer must describe the assignment and its context as much as possible before the tutor can offer feedback that is genuinely helpful.

Promoting Dialogue in Diagnostic and Instructional Comments

The following example reveals the degree of dialogue that an online conference can generate with a writer.

> ****OK, so your argument is that Reich is generally incorrect in his perception of the impact of foreign workers on the U.S. economy, right? I understand your desire to include in the first paragraph every aspect and detail of his argument, but this is not necessary. In your intro you want to lay out general information about Reich's argument and then set up your thesis, which in this case opposes that argument. Later in your paper you can point by point counter his argument. Also be careful of overwhelming the reader with too many quotes in your intro. While these quotes are probably quite useful to your paper, you can sprinkle them throughout the body of the paper.****

The tutor begins with an opening question, used to summarize what she thinks is the writer's main goal. The question, indeed a rhetorical question, expects no response. Rather, it suggests an openness, a give-and-take between writer and tutor, but surely provides a foundational point of initial discussion. If the tutor gets the topic wrong, the remaining critique and tutorial is undermined. Stated as a question, however, the observation remains negotiable, a misunderstanding possibly due to the reader's interpretation rather than cued by the text. Such possibility provides the writer a common ground with the tutor, an ethos of process shared between them if not entirely a mutual understanding of a piece of writing. The uncertainty expressed in the rhetorical nature of the question indicates the tutor's intention to proceed with an open mind. The next few sentences following the rhetorical question contribute in the way Donald Murray described as "the self proposes, the other self considers"[5] or what Kenneth Bruffee refers to as reflective thought.[6] The tutor's tone is cautionary and invites the writer to reconsider his assumptions about what a good opening approach might be.

In a typical tutoring session peer tutors read a paper aloud, stopping now and then to examine troublesome areas in the text. This puts the tutor in control—and the student on the spot. But the goal for learning theorists who advocate a Socratic approach is to engage the learner, not to manipulate him. Ideally, the tutor asks questions before giving directions and engages the client's own knowledge to solve a problem. Emily Meyer and Louise Smith relate some of the background to this theorizing. They explain writing to be a dialogic process within the mind of the writer, especially the experienced writer. Through conversation, the tutor helps the writer to initiate, recognize, and cultivate the dialogic process used by experienced writers. Online tutors can also use questions to engage writers in this exercise.[7] Because the tutor is not waiting for an answer, the writer is free to act as she wishes. The door to genuine contemplation is open and the writer remains in control.

Questions can serve yet another purpose, and that is to soften criticism. Once again, in the absence of facial expression and voice modulation, the tutor must make points clearly but not coldly, as in this example:

> ****I think that you have explained your opinion well in this paragraph. My only concern for content here is, does a job as a bank teller pay the equivalent as an aerobics instructor? Or does working the line in a factory provide better benefits (i.e., health insurance)? These are things to think about when making very generalized comparisons. Generally aerobics instructors don't work full-time nor do they receive health benefits. I understand what it is that you're doing with this example, but I think that the comparison is unfair. Just something to think about.****

This comment occurs later in the paper and works as a probe intended to create dialogue within the writer's mind. In classic fashion, the tutor begins with a compliment before raising a criticism. The criticism is presented as a question, not rhetorical this time but genuine, and, should the writer care to consider it, one which points out a fundamental weakness in the paper: in this case, the writer has made a number of loose, poorly developed correlations. Note the tutor's comment about "when making very generalized comparisons" and how this invites the writer to again share a perspective with the tutor. Here, the tutor has established a foundation for interpretation from which the writer can, by his own will and skill, determine a path of revision. "Well, I'm not trying for very generalized comparisons," he might say. "Why would she say that I'm doing that?" "What does she mean that aerobics instructors don't work full-time? That wasn't my point." And so the dialogue goes. Online tutoring cannot monitor the direction in which the dialogue unfolds or the decisions a writer makes on the basis of it—more on this later. But then, no true collaborator would wish to do that either.

Limiting and Focusing Comments on Grammar and Mechanics

Writing center tutors probably get more requests for help with grammar and mechanics than anything else. What is the best way to respond? Consider this comment from an online tutor:

> ****Two mechanics notes: 1. You want a comma between "agrees" and "explaining," just to make sure the reader doesn't read agreesexplaining, all fast like that. The comma tells the reader to pause. 2. Did you add the word "whom" to Reich's quotation? If so, you should enclose it in [brackets]. (Do that any time you add a word to clarify the meaning of a quotation.) And, because that word represents the subject of a subordinate clause, it should be "who," not "whom."****

In responding online, the tutor has to make a special effort not to correct every error that comes along (see Brooks' "Minimalist Marking" [1995] for more on this matter; also see Chapter 16). Anyone who has ever seen an online paper that has been meticulously corrected will immediately recognize the problem: with all the insertions of asterisks, question marks, boldface words, and underlines, the paper looks as though it has been worked over. It is ironic that painstakingly correcting every error makes a tutor feel exhausted, while the student who receives the corrected paper feels ashamed. This is not conducive to learning. Comments inserted into the body of the text and set off by asterisks or other marks ($ or % or #) can also seem like litter if they occur too often. On the other hand, email attachment files make it possible to use a word processor like Microsoft Word to insert comments in textboxes or in hidden pop-up boxes and to identify edits with the Track Changes feature or by using a different font color; these look much less intrusive on the page.

Students learn in many ways. Irene Lurkis Clark's essay "Collaboration and Ethics in Writing Center Pedagogy"[8] reminds us that imitation has a long history as a prominent way of learning. Citing Lev Vygotsky, she says that human beings "can imitate a variety of actions that go well beyond the limits of their own capabilities."[9] In my example, the tutor advises the writer about specific points of grammar and mechanics, correcting and to some degree explaining the logic behind the change. In this example the tutor takes a directive approach and, in its most extreme fashion so far, renders the tutor in the role of proofreader or editor. And yet, the tutor is striking a balance by holding corrections to a minimum (even though there were many other surface errors in this paper) and supplying them with explanation. While this may be no different than it would be when handled in a face-to-face tutoring session, the online forum can do one thing the face-to-face session cannot, and it again involves email attachments. With an attachment, the tutor can insert a hotlink to a Web page that addresses the specific error in question. The writer can then just click on the link and read all about it.[10] (In a face-to-face session, the equivalent would be to tear a page from a handbook and staple it to the writer's draft.)

Consider how another tutor responded to text-level features in the same student's paper. Notice the less directive approach regarding grammar and mechanics:

> ***Also I would like to suggest that you go back and read your paper aloud to yourself. There are a few places where you have pluralized nouns that should be singular or tacked on an "s" to an adjective. These are relatively easy to find when you read through OUT LOUD. Silent skimming does not catch such mistakes, nor does spell-check.***

Responding in this way, the tutor recommends the "read aloud" scenario used in face-to-face tutoring. (Note that although the tutor just wanted to emphasize the importance of reading aloud by using all caps, it looks like she is shouting. Our recommendation is, when responding online, AVOID ALL CAPS!) Accompanying the suggestion to read aloud is an indication of what the student might find in doing this, clueing him without telling him directly what to fix. In this way, the tutor avoids the pressure to edit a paper and instead transfers the responsibility of making simple corrections back to the student.

When students submit papers containing many errors, tutors can feel obligated to address each problem as it occurs. This process is time-consuming online, pedagogically unsound, and detracts from the tutors' ability to address more global issues. Instead, tutors should locate a pattern of technical errors and use only one or two examples to demonstrate how to correct the problem. In essence, the tutor attempts to teach clients how to recognize and edit errors on their own. In the most severe cases, clients are urged to seek face-to-face help.

Creating Closure with a Final Summation

You will recognize the nature of this end comment. Teachers typically write such a remark at the end of a paper. In the online situation, it provides closure to the session.

> ****The overall structure of your paper is good, with ideas flowing from one another. Really what I'd like to see as a reader is more development of your ideas, especially that part at the end about education and gender equality. You can admit that it'll be a difficult transition period, but it's inevitable and in the end will be better than the current situation. I think that's the reaction I was trying to explain when you were talking about aerobics instructors. The paper looks good grammatically; do try to read it over to check for word choice (*aboard/abroad*) type stuff the spell-check can't catch. Good luck with your revisions.****

Murphy and Sherwood say that the concluding stage "contributes to students' feelings of empowerment, providing them with the confidence they need to take the insights they have gained and apply them in new writing situations."[11] In a face-to-face conference this may be done by asking the student to write a brief evaluation note on what the conference accomplished. Online, this task is left to the tutor, but such a closing doesn't attempt to cover everything. In the example, the tutor begins by praising what is good about the paper and then reiterates a concern raised earlier about the development of ideas. In a directive manner, she briefly sketches out how the development might unfold. The client should leave this conference as he would a face-to-face conference, with a sense of confidence and a solid foundation from which he can proceed into the next draft.

Complicating Matters

Inevitably, the advice we offer will be complicated by the actual tutoring sessions you will encounter. Whether our advice—or any advice—works can only be determined by feedback from the writers themselves, and this can be hard to come by in the online environment. Despite all the strategies tutors use to

re-create a dialogue online, one element of conversation remains irrecover-
able—body language. Unlike a face-to-face conference, when an OWL tutor
sends a finished conference back to a client there is no way to gauge the
success of the conference. Harris agrees that "nodding, smiling to show agreement, and offering other small but significant human gestures of friendliness
and approval are additional means of conveying our messages" and are important for communication feedback.[12] OWL tutors cannot monitor the client's
understanding or receptiveness to their suggestions without such feedback.

Occasionally the tutor has a chance to see the writer's revision. When the
tutor examines changes in the revision, the tutor must make assumptions about
the motivations behind each change or lack of change. For example, Morton
(our writer) sent our OWL two revisions of his Reich paper, but each version
was very similar to the previous one despite requests by three different tutors
for more drastic improvements in content, logic, and development. Specifically, the tutors felt that the introduction contained too many quotes, some
examples were inappropriate, and his final argument barely supported his thesis. The tutors determined that Morton ignored their suggestions for major
revisions in favor of the easier sentence-level corrections.

An interview with Morton revealed that he was a very independent writer,
looking for feedback more than actual help in writing his paper. He was very
concerned with clarity but was confident about what he had to say. According to
Morton, one of the OWL's best assets is the opportunity to have more than one
person critique the same paper. He anticipated that each tutor would have a different style and would offer different ideas—exactly what he wanted. He
ignored the tutors' critiques of his introduction, however, because in class discussions his instructor praised students who used quotes. He did attempt to find
better examples for his arguments but said he did not have the time nor the
research skills to find stronger support. As for his concluding argument, Morton
felt that he made sufficient changes to clarify that section of his paper. These
three OWL conferences combined with his own optimistic opinion of his writing convinced Morton that he would earn an A. His instructor gave him a B–.

Morton was upset and angry. He reported that none of the criticisms his
instructor made about the paper coincided with the tutors' comments. She
loved his introduction, he said, but she did not feel that his arguments related
to his thesis. Overall, Morton did not agree with the teacher's comments or
what she felt to be good writing.

From the tutors' points of view, had Morton more carefully considered
their comments he might have done better on the paper. Indeed, the fact that
the teacher felt the arguments were not related to the thesis indicated to our
tutors that they were on to something when they questioned the appropriateness of his reasoning and examples. Moreover, as revealed in the interview,
Morton appeared to have been poised from the beginning not to make whole-
sale changes. His confidence "about what he had to say" may have inured him
against really listening (in this case, reading) closely to what his tutors were

telling him. But this is not unique to tutoring, online or in person. Plenty of suggestions are not heard in face-to-face tutoring and plenty of connections are nodded to but not really made. The refusal of a suggestion is perhaps the most significant form of empowerment that a student can make. It might also be argued that online tutoring makes such empowerment even more likely to occur, accompanied as it is by an absence of social pressure.

The most salient aspect of success, if we can draw one from the conference with Morton, has to do with his wanting feedback. He wanted to share in some kind of conversation. Although he claimed that the conferences were too specific to affect his future writing and that to him, the tutors' comments were out of sync with what his teacher wanted, it is not at all clear what will actually unfold as he writes more. He asked for feedback and he got it. Like many students, Morton possessed at this moment a pragmatic goal—to get a good grade, and that is why he went to our peer tutors. Nonetheless, each tutor had a different (and not-so-different) take on his paper, and he wanted to experience all of them, regardless of whether he chose to internalize or employ this particular advice. Each of us knows from our own experience that human beings sometimes suppress advice and remember it later in life. This, too, is a significant feature of learning; we will learn when we are ready to learn, not before.

More significant than a revision of any one paper is to observe whether students continue to submit papers for feedback. (Despite Morton's initial disappointment in his grade, he still sends his papers to our OWL.) Even if our clients do not respond to every suggestion we deem important, they retain their independence as writers to pick and choose how they would like to revise. When clients leave conferences confident enough to take advantage of that independence, when they use the service repeatedly, whether for informal feedback or because they are committed to using the advice they are given, the OWL can maintain and even expand the valuable principles of collaborative teaching and learning.

Further Reading

Coogan, David, ed. 1999. *Electronic Writing Centers.* Stamford, CT: Ablex.

This book takes the long view of electronic tutoring and what it means for the future of learning to write. The first chapter, "Tutors and Computers in Composition Studies," invites us "to look beyond the roles that writing centers have lovingly constructed for the tutor and the writer" so that today's writing centers will continue to be a force in literacy learning in the future.

Dayton, David. 1998. "Technical Editing Online: The Quest for Transparent Technology." *Journal of Technical Writing and Communication* 28 (1): 4–37.

This article will be of interest to online tutors who work with technical papers. The author reviews discussions of online editing in the field of technical communication; he tries to explain how online editing has been shaped within the field and why many technical editors remain loyal to traditional paper-based procedures. Explaining advantages and disadvantages of various software used in online editing, the author reports that online procedures fundamentally change traditional editing. He argues that their use and development is inevitable and ought to be approached both critically and with an open mind.

Harris, Muriel, and Michael Pemberton. 1995. "Online Writing Labs (OWLs): A Taxonomy of Options and Issues." *Computers and Composition* 12 (2): 145–59.

Available on CD, this guide contains a wide range of topics, including video clips on starting an OWL, training tutors, and even writing grants to fund OWL projects.

Hobson, Eric, ed. 1998. *Wiring the Writing Center.* Logan: Utah State University Press.

A helpful and informative collection of essays that shows the ingenuity and commitment of writing center colleagues as they implement technology in writing classes. Although advocating the use of online technologies in writing centers, the collection also addresses broad and daunting issues of the costs of going online, both economic and pedagogical.

Inman, James, and Clinton Gardner, eds. 2002. *The OWL Construction and Maintenance Guide.* Emmitsburg, MD: IWCA Press.

Rafoth, Ben. 2004. "Tutoring ESL Papers Online." In *ESL Writers: A Guide for Writing Center Tutors,* eds. Shanti Bruce and Ben Rafoth. Portsmouth, NH: Boynton/Cook, 94–104.

When it comes to giving feedback, less is more in some cases where students submit their papers online. See how a tutor's comment is improved as it becomes shorter and more focused.

Notes

1. Andrea Lunsford, "Collaboration, Control, and the Idea of a Writing Center," *Writing Center Journal* 12 (1) (1991): 8.

2. Barbara Monroe, "The Look and Feel of the OWL Conference," in *Wiring the Writing Center,* ed. Eric Hobson (Logan: Utah State University Press, 1998), 23.

3. Muriel Harris, *Teaching One-to-One: The Writing Conference* (Urbana, IL: NCTE, 1986), 41.

4. Harris, 41–43.

5. Donald Murray, "Teaching the Other Self: The Writer's First Reader," *College Composition and Communication* 33 (1982): 140.

6. Kenneth Bruffee, "Collaborative Learning and the 'Conversation of Mankind,'" *College English* 46 (1978): 639.

7. Emily Meyer and Louise Smith, *The Practical Tutor* (Oxford: Oxford University Press, 1987), 31–32.

8. Irene L. Clark, "Collaboration and Ethics in Writing Center Pedagogy," in *The St. Martin's Sourcebook for Writing Tutors,* eds. Christina Murphy and Steve Sherwood (New York: St. Martin's), 88.

9. Clark, 92.

10. The online writing center at Indiana University of Pennsylvania is an example of an OWL that uses attachment technology to insert hotlinks into the student's online paper.

11. In Meyer and Smith, 14.

12. Harris, 43.

Works Cited

Brooks, J. 1995. "Minimalist Marking." In *The St. Martin's Sourcebook for Writing Tutors,* eds. C. Murphy and S. Sherwood, 83–87. New York: St. Martin's.

Bruffee, K. 1984. "Collaborative Learning and the 'Conversation of Mankind.'" *College English* 46 (7): 635–52.

Clark, I. L. 1995. "Collaboration and Ethics in Writing Center Pedagogy." *The St. Martin's Sourcebook for Writing Tutors,* eds. C. Murphy and S. Sherwood, 88–95. New York: St. Martin's.

Harris, M. 1986. *Teaching One-to-One: The Writing Conference.* Urbana, IL: NCTE.

Lunsford, A. 1991. "Collaboration, Control, and the Idea of a Writing Center." *Writing Center Journal* 12 (1): 3–10.

Meyer, E., and L. Smith. 1987. *The Practical Tutor.* Oxford: Oxford University Press.

Monroe, B. 1998. "The Look and Feel of the OWL Conference." In *Wiring the Writing Center,* ed. E. Hobson, 3–24. Logan: Utah State University Press.

Murphy, C., and S. Sherwood. 1995. "The Tutoring Process: Exploring Paradigms and Practices." In *The St. Martin's Sourcebook for Writing Tutors,* eds. C. Murphy and S. Sherwood, 1–17. New York: St. Martin's.

Murray, D. 1982. "Teaching the Other Self: The Writer's First Reader." *College Composition and Communication* 33: 140–47.

16

Can You Proofread This?

Beth Rapp Young[1]

Anyone who works in a writing center becomes familiar with requests like, "My paper is due in forty-five minutes—can someone here proofread it for me?" With imposing urgency, some writers expect tutors to give the paper absolution and a quick blessing. Tutors risk disappointing students when they explain that they cannot comb through a paper for errors, mark and correct each one, and hand the paper back with a stamp of approval. There is another kind of risk as well, and this one stems from the very idea of correctness in writing. What's correct? Who is to judge? Why does it matter? Some writing centers try to stay away from proofreading altogether. Yet the fact is, students enter most writing centers expecting to receive help on all aspects of their writing, including final editing. This chapter offers thoughts on why proofreading is a dilemma in itself, and then—for those who struggle with it—some ways to help writers proofread their own papers.

Experienced tutors understand that when writers ask us to proofread, they may really be asking, "What do you think of my ideas?" "Have I supported my point?" or "Does it flow?" Careful questioning is important when working with a writer you've never assisted before. What many tutors don't realize is that the decision to proofread requires a shared understanding between the tutor and writer, one that recognizes the problems inherent in bringing papers to the writing center for proofreading. The first step, therefore, is always to be alert to the possibility that the writer may ask for help with grammar or proofreading when he actually wants something different but doesn't know how to ask for it. So if there is an opportunity to talk about ideas, take it and leave the proofreading for later. After all, once the writer changes the ideas and sentences, proofreading must begin all over again.

What about when the writer says, "I feel very good about the ideas and the organization—I've shown it to other writing consultants and other people in the class, and I've incorporated their suggestions for revision. Plus, this paper is due in an hour. So I need someone to look it over and see if there are any errors"? Should you tell that writer that she has come to the wrong place?

Some would argue that proofreading is against the purpose of writing centers because writing centers are supposed to work toward better writers, not better papers (for a famous example of this dictum, see North [1984]). Another argument is that proofreading supports an unrealistic view of writing-as-product, not process. Proofreading does this by ignoring the global revision needs of a paper in favor of error checking, especially when the writer still needs to work on ideas and organization. (Clark [1998] compares too-early proofreading to polishing fifty pieces of wood before you know which pieces you'll use to build a table. Obviously, building the table should come before polishing it.)

Finally, some worry that an emphasis on proofreading will transform the experience of working in a writing center. Rather than focusing on the writer, writing consultants will need to focus on the text. Will writing consultants enjoy proofreading as much as the other work? And what if they miss an error or two? Will the writer hold the writing center responsible? Will writers even bother to proofread if they know someone skilled at writing can do it for them? And what message does *that* send? Questions such as these illuminate potential risks associated with proofreading. Each writing center should try to define its own purpose and mission in ways that recognize these risks.

One way to understand proofreading is in terms of the writing process. How can a writing center be complete, providing help from invention to revision, if it doesn't pay full attention to that final step? Arguably, ignoring something that matters to most readers gives an unrealistic view of the writer's obligation to her reader and creates the impression that correctness doesn't matter. Besides, writers learn from modeling. When we say, "We can't proofread for you, but we'll teach you how to proofread your own paper," there is an opportunity here to show the writer how good proofreaders work. Part of the argument for writing centers is that an outside reader can notice things the writer cannot because he is too familiar with the paper. Writers can learn from tutors how to step back from the piece and see it with fresh eyes. Finally, let's remember that writers may visit the center for proofreading but return for other kinds of help. Proofreading may just be the entrée.

Some Background

A large body of research on errors and correction in writing provides different perspectives on this issue. While some have tried to classify the different types of errors and determine which ones occur most frequently (Connors and Lunsford 1988), others have examined the effects that various errors have on readers' attitudes (Hairston 1981; Hull 1985). Modern approaches to error have been more inclined to follow Mina Shaughnessy's (1977) lead and regard error as a natural part of learning the skill of writing. When viewed this way, errors are not always straightforward mistakes. Sometimes they are the result of an incorrect or misapplied rule that the writer has learned, or they may be caused by intrusions from the writer's spoken language (or her first language, in the case of second language writers).[2] And sometimes they lie in the eye of the beholder. In a 1981 article in the journal *College Composition and Communication,* author Joseph Williams slyly inserted about one hundred errors—typos, misspellings, repetitions, and so on—into his article on error, but few readers (college English teachers mostly) caught on until the author told them at the end what he had done. His purpose was to demonstrate that English teachers find numerous errors in student writing because they are looking for them, and where they do not expect to find them, they don't, even when they are plainly there.

Errors are no joke in most teachers' minds, however, and students are justifiably concerned about the impact that errors will have on their grade. Helping a writer to proofread can be tremendously valuable when it is done for the purpose of teaching the student to find her own errors. Tutors may pride themselves on doing this well. Some writing centers approach the issue as a research problem by first listing all of the errors and then studying them with the writer to see what they have in common. In the long list of possible errors writers make, it is worth noting that readers tend to be bothered more by some than others—usually sentence-level problems (run ons and fragments), excessive commas, and nonparallel constructions (Cazort 1997; Hairston 1981).

What to Do

Beginning tutors may be tempted to plunge right in, but experienced tutors know that proofreading is rarely a straightforward process. Here are some general strategies to bear in mind. (Near the end of this section, you will see some specific suggestions for helping writers.)

First, talk with the writer about proofreading before you begin and decide whether it is necessary at this time. If so, be honest about your own limitations and don't allow yourself to be framed as a writing expert; this would be a no-win situation for both of you. It is better to treat the problems you are unsure about as curiosities, and you will be surprised at how often the real answer is that there is no single correct answer. This is not because there are no correct answers. Rather, many of the questions that writers express involve aspects of language usage that have more than one right answer. This is another reason why it is important to understand that proofreading is not a straightforward business and that editing decisions are ultimately the writer's responsibility.

Experienced tutors don't attempt to pick out every mistake they see. Instead, they look for error patterns. You and the writer can then decide which errors to work on. Spelling, for example, might be something the writer feels he can correct on his own or with spell check. Software such as MLA's *Editor* may help with error analysis. Use grammar checkers with caution, though, because they identify many "errors" that aren't errors at all (like passive voice) and they fail to catch errors that really are (like agreement). Look for grammar checkers that print a comprehensive list of errors, rather than requiring you to address each error one at a time. The comprehensive printout can be reassuring because what looks like eighty-five individual errors with a standard grammar checker may turn out to be only four patterns of error. Nonetheless, many writing centers avoid grammar and style checkers altogether because of the mixed messages they can create.

Remember to make errors the writer is most concerned about a priority. You can determine this by asking questions about errors that have been marked in earlier papers, those that seem to be especially annoying to the instructor (sexist language, perhaps), or that will be fatal for that assignment ("any paper with two or more sentence fragments will fail"). For writers worried about questions that have no clear right-or-wrong answers, it may be best to focus on matters of voice, tone, consistency, or purpose as a way of deciding what to do.

In your discussions, don't be afraid to turn to a handbook! Writers are sometimes unsure about how to use handbooks effectively, so when you turn to a handbook you model an important skill that writers can learn to use on their own. Beginning tutors sometimes worry that consulting a handbook hurts their credibility, but actually, demonstrating that you know how to use writerly resources enhances your credibility at the same time that it helps you resist being framed as the authority. In fact, it's often useful to consult more than one handbook because different handbooks explain concepts differently, yielding a fuller understanding of the issue. Sometimes handbooks even disagree, and that disagreement can help a writer stop seeking *the* correct answer and start considering which strategy is best for her particular paper. Consulting handbooks is a great way for tutors and writers to learn more about language and how it works.

Finally, I recommend that tutors look for opportunities to learn about language and how it works. Read and write often, paying attention to how authors convey different tones and experimenting with new styles in your own writing (see Chapter 9). A heightened sense of curiosity about writing is what many tutors point to when they say that working in the writing center taught them more about writing than they could have learned in any class.

Regardless of the general approach you use, here are some specific techniques tutors can use to help writers with proofreading:

- *Explain how you find errors.* In other words, do your best to think out loud to help the writer learn from your example.

- *Explain suggestions according to the writer's intended meaning.* ("With the commas, it sounds like you mean . . ." or "When you change tenses, I can't tell if you mean . . .").

  Also, remember that rules are made to be broken and what the writer is doing may be creative and effective even if he doesn't fully understand it. Be open to this, and talk with the writer about whether it works. If you are both unsure, seek another opinion.

- *Compare specific strong and weak examples from the paper.* ("You use passive voice in this sentence, but over here, you use active voice. See how this sentence is less wordy?")
- *Let the writer try out strategies on his own.* ("OK, I've shown you how to change this sentence to remove the dangling modifier. How would you fix this next dangling modifier?")
- *Maintain a healthy sense of doubt.* ("This might be wrong—I tend to get mixed up about *lie/lay*. Have you brought your handbook?") A tutor isn't expected to be The Grammar God. Tutors are expected to help writers learn to help themselves. Modeling use of a handbook is a great way to do that. Maintain doubt also by asking gently, "Why did you do this?" The answer may reveal that the writer is laboring under a misconception—or, it may reveal that you have misunderstood his intention.

At the end of this chapter (see Appendix A), you will find a list of techniques writers and tutors can use to check quickly for ideas and organization before embarking on proofreading (also see Chapter 11, for more on organization). You will also find a list of proofreading techniques to use in locating surface errors (see Appendix B), a table that tries to match techniques with writing problems (see Appendix C), and suggested guidelines for prioritizing errors (see Appendix D). Use them as a guide for reflecting on various approaches to helping writers with their proofreading.

Complicating Matters

So it's as easy as that? Well, it's probably not that easy. In practice, these strategies have mixed results. Here are some of the difficulties we've run into in the writing center where I work. How would you address them?

Writers may regard the writing center as a place to share the burden. They may feel resentment and think, "I don't know this stuff. I did all I can do and now I've come here for help, not to be told to do it myself. If I could do it myself, I wouldn't need to come here." Given the great amount of time some writers invest in ideas, research, and revising, isn't it fair for them to ask the writing center to proofread for them so that they can devote more of their time to ideas, research, and revision?

Many writing centers have embraced the goal of empowering *student writers* to become *writers,* which involves, in part, helping students to learn the practices and habits of writers with *real-world* audiences and goals. Yet in the workplace and other so-called real-world settings, writers often turn to someone else for help with proofreading, because outside readers are more effective proofreaders. In fact, research by Glynda Hull (1985) examined just this point. Hull asked groups of more-skilled and less-skilled college writers to proofread several essays, some of which were written by others, some of which were written by the the writers in the study. Hull found that more-skilled writers were better than less-skilled writers at proofreading papers written by someone else. But the two groups performed about the same when proofreading their own work—neither group corrected many errors at all. If proofreading is best done by someone other than the writer, should a writing center offer to proofread for writers, rather than helping writers learn how to proofread for themselves?

Writers may not know enough to share the burden. Some writers may honestly not be able to find errors themselves. For example, ESL writers who come to the writing center for help with articles and prepositions are often unable to locate problems with these words (see Chapter 7). Even when we try our best to explain the rules, ESL writers may not be able to spot problems with articles. This is because many languages do not have articles (those that do often use them differently from English), and because the rules for article use in English are surprisingly complex. One ESL speaker, a Japanese-born college professor, noted, "I have studied articles for seventeen years, and I am finally beginning to feel I've mastered them."[3] As this professor knew, ESL writers need practice and experience to acquire a good sense of articles. Thirty minutes, even with careful explanation, isn't likely to make a big difference. How can a tutor know how much progress is realistic to expect in a proofreading session?

Some errors may be a normal side effect of writing improvement. As writers experiment with new techniques, it stands to reason that they will make mistakes while they are learning to master those techniques. To test this theory, Richard H. Haswell (1988) compared the errors made by college freshmen, sophomores, juniors, and postcollege employees. He found that college students' writing did improve, and that they continued to make mistakes at the same rate while they were improving, but the mistakes were allied to the improvement. For example, as college students learned to write more complex sentences, they would make new mistakes that could not be made in simpler sentences. One implication of Haswell's finding is that undue effort to prevent the mistakes may also hinder the improvement. Given this, how much effort should a tutor spend on helping writers correct mistakes?

A student had worked diligently on a paper with one of the tutors in our writing center, only to return after she had received a C grade. At the bottom of her paper, the instructor wrote, "Next time, proofread!" Though the student did not try to blame the tutor, she was clearly discouraged. And the tutor felt terrible because he had not recognized several major errors in the paper. What would you say to this tutor? What should the tutor say to the student?

Further Reading

Bishop, Wendy, ed. 1997. *Elements of Alternate Style*. Portsmouth, NH: Boynton/Cook.

If ever a book made the point that rules of grammar and proper usage were made to be broken, this is it. Various authors contribute chapters to this book covering such topics as fractured narratives, risk taking, radical revision, and alternative grammars. This is a delightful read for anyone who has thought about breaking conventions creatively, and a must for anyone in danger of becoming too serious about correctness.

Hartwell, Patrick. 1985. "Grammar, Grammars, and the Teaching of Grammar." *College English* 47: 105–27.

In all that has been written about grammar and the teaching of writing, this article is a standout for the clarity with which it frames the debate. Hartwell explains the various meanings of grammar and why matters of usage, correctness, and style are fundamentally different from linguistics and the language we all acquire as we grow up. This article also helps in understanding why research findings have shown that grammar instruction in school does not tend to improve writing.

Linville, Cynthia. 2004. "Editing Line by Line." In *ESL Writers: A Guide for Writing Center Tutors*, eds. Shanti Bruce and Ben Rafoth, 84–93. Portsmouth, NH: Boynton/Cook.

ESL writers often want to know the rule behind every correction, while tutors often don't know the rule or can't verbalize it. This chapter helps tutors deal with word- and sentence-level errors that arise in tutoring sessions with ESL as well as native English–speaking writers.

Notes

1. This chapter began as a presentation at the National Conference on Peer Tutoring in Writing, The State University of New York at Plattsburgh, Nov. 6–8, 1998.
2. David Bartholomae, "The Study of Error," *College Composition and Communication* 31 (October 1980): 253–69.
3. *English Composition for Non-native Speakers,* videotape, (Miami: University of Miami, 1996).

Works Cited

Bartholomae, D. 1980. "The Study of Error." *College Composition and Communication* 31: 253–69.

Cazort, D. 1997. *Under the Grammar Hammer: The 25 Most Important Grammar Mistakes and How to Avoid Them.* Los Angeles: Lowell House.

Clark, I. L. 1998. *Writing in the Center.* 3d ed. Dubuque, IA: Kendall/Hunt.

Connors, R. J., and A. A. Lunsford. 1988. "Frequency of Formal Errors in Current College Writing, or Ma & Pa Kettle Do Research." *College Composition and Communication* 39: 395–409.

English Composition for Non-native Speakers. 1996. Videotape. Miami: University of Miami.

Hairston, M. 1981. "Not All Errors Are Created Equal: Nonacademic Readers in the Professions Respond to Lapses in Usage." *College English* 41: 794–806.

Haswell, R. H. 1988. "Error and Change in Student Writing." *Written Communication* 5: 479–99.

Hull, G. 1985. "Research on Error and Correction." In *Perspectives on Research and Scholarship in Composition,* eds. B. McClelland and T. Donovan, 162–84. New York: Modern Language Association.

North, S. 1984. "The Idea of a Writing Center." *College English* 46 (5): 433–46.

Shaughnessy, M. 1977. *Errors and Expectations.* New York: Oxford.

Williams, J. 1981. "The Phenomenology of Error." *College Composition and Communication* 32: 152–68.

Appendix A

Global Techniques Writers and Tutors Can
Use for Ideas and Organization

Before beginning to proofread for surface errors, look carefully at ideas and organization.

Underline the thesis.

Is there a thesis? Where is it? Does it accurately reflect the paper? Is it interesting, or is it a just-add-water, three-part boring thesis? If the writer agrees the ideas are weak, help the writer make a plan to contact the instructor and ask for an extension to start over.

Help the writer create a descriptive outline for the paper.

What does each paragraph or section do? What does the paper as a whole do? It is one thing to know *what a paragraph says,* but just as important to know *what it does* to strengthen the paper.

Underline transitions between paragraphs.

Are there enough transitions? Do the transitions help to connect the paragraphs to the thesis? Do the transitions show how different paragraphs relate to each other, or do they just mark items in a list ("One thing . . . and another thing . . . and another thing . . .")?

Work with the writer to create an abstract of the paper.

Start with the thesis and condense each paragraph to one sentence. If this proves to be too difficult to do, you may have located a problem with paragraph coherence. Fit all of this into one paragraph. Is it clear how each idea leads to the next? Is the abstract coherent? If not, revise the abstract. Next, using the abstract as a guide, revise the paper.

Underline each important idea in a different color. Then underline information related to each idea in the same color.

Is supporting material located near the idea it is supposed to support? Can you see a pattern in the arrangement of this information, or is everything mixed together?

Examine suspect paragraphs (unusually long, unusually short, can't tell what it does in a descriptive outline, can't condense to a sentence, etc.) by assigning a level of generality to each sentence.

Too many level-one sentences? No level-one sentences? Enough level-two and level-three sentences to support each level-one?

Underline the new or important information in each sentence.

Is this information located near stress points? We usually stress the words before or after a pause, especially at the end of the sentence. It-clefts ("It is interesting to . . ."), that-clefts ("That a problem arose is . . .") and there transformations ("There is a consensus . . .") can create additional stress points. Does information already provided or a transitional cue ("By contrast," "What is more," "Despite this fact," etc.) prepare readers for new information?

Appendix B

Proofreading Techniques Writers and Tutors Can Use for Surface Features

Get a Fresh Perspective

• Take a break (as little as five minutes) between writing and proofreading.

• Ask someone to read the paper to you, or read the paper to someone else.

• Read the paper into a tape recorder; play back the tape while you follow along.

• Listen for:

  1. Places where what is read differs from what is written
  2. Places where the reader stumbles for any reason
  3. Places where the listener gets distracted, confused, or bored

Slow Down

• Cover the writing with a ruler or piece of paper so you can see only one line of text at a time.

• Read backward, sentence by sentence (for unclear sentence structure, redundancy).

• Read backward, word by word (for typos and spelling mistakes).

• Circle verbs (to locate passive voice, strong verbs, tense shifts).

• Circle prepositional phrases (to locate wordiness).

• Point at punctuation marks as you name each piece of a citation (for proper citation format; for example, "Last name comma year. Date colon page numbers.")

Personalize the Process

• Help the writer to begin an editing checklist of frequent mistakes. Keep the checklist for use with subsequent papers. Update it every time a paper is returned.

• Read through the paper several times, looking for a different problem each time.

Use a Computer

• Print a draft designed especially for proofreading.

- Doublespace the text. Put in extra hard returns so that each sentence starts on a new line (to locate fragments).

- Use 14-point or larger type (for apostrophe and comma problems).

- Use the find/replace function for items on your editing checklist, including wordiness flags ("to be" verbs, prepositions, etc.) and typos (*from/ form*, extra spaces after periods, unnecessary commas, etc.).

- Use spell check and grammar check software. These programs are hardly foolproof, but when interpreted with a tutor who is a good editor, they can be helpful.

- Tell the writer about good online grammar websites and telephone hotlines. These can usually be found by visiting writing center home pages on the Internet.

Appendix C

Proofreading Techniques

These proofreading techniques can help you locate different kinds of problems (right).	Spelling	Wrong Word	Incorrect Citation Format	Verb Tense Problems	Subject-Verb Agreement	Pronoun Agreement	Misplaced Modifiers
Take a break before proofreading.	X	X	X	X	X	X	X
Print a proofreading draft with extra space in margins and doublespace text.	X	X	X	X	X	X	X
Create a personalized editing checklist based on your previous writing.	X	X	X	X	X	X	X
Read paper more than once, looking for a different problem each time.	X	X	X	X	X	X	X

	1	2	3	4	5	6	7
Read aloud to someone else.				X	X	X	X
Have someone read aloud while you follow along.	X	X	X	X	X		X
Physically cover up all but the line you're reading.	X	X	X				
Read backward, word by word.	X						
Read backward, sentence by sentence.	X	X	X	X	X	X	X
Point at words as you read them aloud to yourself.	X	X					
Circle all verbs, then check for tense, agreement, voice, mood, and so on.				X	X		X
Circle prepositions, then check for clarity. If possible, reword to eliminate prepositions.							X
Circle commas, then check to see if they are correctly used.							X

Proofreading Techniques (*continued*)

Point at and name punctuation as you read.			X				X
Use find/replace function to search for likely misspellings or wrong words (e.g., *their/there*).	X	X					
Use spell check software. (Warning: This software won't catch all errors.)	X						
Use grammar check software. (Warning: This software won't catch all errors and is frequently incorrect.)	X			X	X		

These proofreading techniques can help you locate different kinds of problems (right).	Sentence Fragments	Comma Splices	General Punctuation Problems	Wordiness	Linear Coherence ("Flow")	Paragraph Structure	Support of Ideas	Overall Organization	Thesis
Take a break before proofreading.	X	X	X	X	X	X	X	X	X
Print a proofreading draft with extra space in margins and doublespace text.	X	X	X	X	X	X	X	X	X
Create a personalized editing checklist based on your previous writing.	X	X	X	X	X	X	X	X	X
Read paper more than once, looking for a different problem each time.	X	X	X	X	X	X	X	X	X
Read aloud to someone else.				X	X		X	X	X

Proofreading Techniques (*continued*)

Have someone read aloud while you follow along.	X	X	X	X	X		X	X
Physically cover up all but the line you're reading.						X		
Read backward, word by word.					X			
Read backward, sentence by sentence.						X	X	
Point at words as you read them aloud to yourself.					X			
Circle all verbs, then check for tense, agreement, voice, mood, and so on.							X	
Circle prepositions, then check for clarity. If possible, reword to eliminate prepositions.					X			

Strategy					
Circle commas, then check to see if they are correctly used.	X	X			
Point at and name punctuation as you read.	X	X			
Use find/replace function to search for likely misspellings or wrong words (e.g., *their/there*).					
Use spell check software. (Warning: This software won't catch all errors.)					
Use grammar check software. (Warning: This software won't catch all errors and is frequently incorrect.)	X	X		X	

Appendix D

Error Priority Guidelines

Remember, you'll need to read the entire paper before you can prioritize errors. Try to focus on errors in this order:

1. Errors that affect comprehension of the text
2. Errors that the writer is especially concerned about
3. Errors that occur again and again
4. Errors that can be fixed by learning a rule
5. Errors that don't violate a particular rule, but rather are matters of idiom or preference

When several different errors fall into the same category, you and the writer should decide which errors to address first. Here are some points to consider as you decide:

- Which errors is the writer interested in or ready to address?
- Which errors are likely to bother readers the most? (You might want to refer to Douglas Cazort's list of "Five Uncommonly Serious Mistakes" in *Under the Grammar Hammer* (1997). You might also ask which errors the teacher has complained about in the past.)
- Which errors are most likely to reappear in future papers?
- Which errors do you feel the most comfortable explaining?

17

Using Others' Words

Quoting, Summarizing, and Documenting Sources

Mary Mortimore Dossin

Many colleges and universities publish plagiarism policies that are harsh and punitive. Words like *theft*, *integrity*, and *character issue* give the issue a moral dimension that calls into question the ethics of individuals who plagiarize. What tutors are more likely to encounter in the writing center, however, are not intentional plagiarists but students who are genuinely befuddled by what Libby Miles terms "the contradictions of American academic writing":

> Show you have done your research *but* write something new and original.
> Appeal to experts and authorities *but* improve upon or disagree with them.
> Improve your English by mimicking what you hear and read *but* use your own words, your own voice.
> Give credit where credit is due *but* make your own significant contribution.[1]

Not an easy course to navigate! Tutors can help.

Some Background

Definitions of plagiarism vary according to time, place, and discipline. The concepts of authorship[2] and originality[3] are attributed to the eighteenth century in Western cultures. Libby Miles writes that other cultures are much less insistent upon careful documenting of sources than American institutions,[4] and Irene L. Clark notes that imitation has had an important role in learning in certain times and cultures.[5] In fact, in Chinese culture, copying classic authors is actually seen as a virtue, a way of honoring those traditional authors, according to Kristin Walker in the *Writing Lab Newsletter*.[6] In addition, Walker found in her work with engineering students—for whom English is a second language—that disciplines also vary in their definitions of plagiarism.[7] (See Chapter 7.)

159

Here and now, however, and in most disciplines, plagiarism is a serious issue that has recently acquired a new twist: the Internet. Students now have abundant opportunities to lift prewritten term papers off of the Web. As well, professors can now subscribe to Internet services like those of Plagiarism.org or Turnitin.com to detect papers copied by their students. The jury is still out on whether the bad guys or the sheriffs will win on this one. In any case, intentional plagiarists are not as frequent in the writing center as are genuinely confused students who want to avoid something about which their professor has given them dire warnings: when viewed in this way, there really are no bad guys and sheriffs.

What to Do

An occasional scene in most writing centers is a student sitting at a computer surrounded by photocopied articles with highlighted passages. She picks up one of the articles, leafs through it, then sets it in front of her and writes a bit on the computer. Then she picks up another and repeats the process. It's slow going. By the time she approaches one of the peer writing tutors to ask about documentation guidelines, it's almost too late. Her chance of producing an honest, original paper has been seriously jeopardized.

Inexperienced researchers, or those who have developed bad habits like those just mentioned, need clarification of the skills demanded by a research paper assignment: gathering information, analyzing and synthesizing the information, and communicating one's own understanding of this information to others. Learning that such skills are essential in the working world can help instill in students the motivation needed to master them. Writing centers need to be proactive rather than just reactive on the issues of research papers. Work-shops and class visits can get out the message about the kind of early work that is necessary for an original paper.

Students need to know that they can come to the writing center for assistance long before they are ready to write a draft of the paper. Plagiarism begins much earlier: when the topic is chosen, when notes are taken (or not taken), and when the analysis and synthesis stage is done (or not done). Writing tutors can be most effective in helping students to avoid plagiarism if they intervene at these early stages.

The first real necessity is a topic the writer cares about. Writing an honest paper is hard work, and students are unlikely to be motivated to invest the energy and curiosity needed unless they have chosen a topic that is truly a question they need to answer for themselves. Talking with a tutor or the pro-fessor at this stage can help the writer discover a topic and an angle to which he can commit himself.

Then, in order to use the words of others effectively and appropriately, the writer must both master his sources and break his connection to their language and structure. There are two necessities for doing these things: taking honest notes and building a structure and language that evolve from the writer's own analysis and synthesis of the information being gathered. Student writers often don't know these requirements or don't have the skills available to follow them effectively. Tutors need to be prepared to help students during these stages in the process.

For the first, copying information directly from sources or highlighting it on a photocopy without taking time to make sense of the information in one's own language will lead to a plagiarized paper no matter how diligent one is about the fine points of documentation style. Honest notes with direct quotations clearly noted and most of the information in the writer's own words will make the writing of an original paper much more likely. The skills of paraphrasing and summarizing are essential for notes. Invaluable and detailed material on these skills (and all other aspects of writing research papers) can be found in Diana Hacker's (1999) *A Writer's Reference* and on the Purdue Online Writing Lab (OWL). The Purdue OWL,[8] for example, has detailed instructions on "Quoting, Paraphrasing, and Summarizing" that first compares and contrasts the terms, then gives an example illustrating their use, and finally offers a sample essay on which to practice these skills. An exercise entitled "Paraphrasing" gives some sample passages on which a writer can practice. In another handout, sample answers to this exercise are given, which a writer can compare to her own work. Tutor assistance with such an exercise would be helpful to those writers for whom the written information is not enough. Doing such work directly with a writer's own sources can also be very useful.

Analysis and synthesis of material is also essential. This stage is often skipped because students don't know it's necessary, haven't allowed time for it, or don't know how to do it. Tutors can help by using the Twenty Questions for Research Writing (Figure 17–1 later in the chapter) to enable a writer to talk or to write her way through this important step. Daily writing—what Peter Elbow (1995) terms "making a mess" in *On Writing*—will help more than anything else. The writer should answer the questions, whether verbally or in writing, in her own language. Set the source aside while the questions are being answered. When this is done, both the language and the structure that evolve as the writer answers the questions will be the writer's own. This work is most beneficial if it is spread out over the several weeks in which the writer is researching her subject. Returning to questions at different stages is useful.

A live body—the tutor—is of enormous benefit at this stage. Nothing beats the presence of another when a writer is wrestling with ideas and striving for new insight. The best gift a tutor can give a writer at this stage is his real curiosity about the topic. Talking writers through this stage will not work if it is a regimented process. Tutors need energy and curiosity as much as writers do. Tutors who are eager to learn more about a wide variety of subjects will be good at this. Their questions will arise naturally out of their own enthusiasm of discovery. Tutors who are just going through the motions will confirm the writer's suspicions that research papers are a tedious and boring exercise in demonstrating command of the conventions of grammar and format.

After honest notes and an original structure have been achieved, the writer is ready to learn about techniques for weaving the words and ideas of others into her own text. The two most common mistakes of unintentional plagiarists are failing to cite paraphrased material and failing to put language from the source into quotation marks. Here, too, tutors can help by pointing out useful written material that clearly illustrates ways of using the others' words and ideas appropriately. Once again, reach for Hacker (1999). In her section on research writing, the author includes principles and examples on integrating information from sources. Sections on using signal phrases give helpful examples. There are also rules and examples on using ellipsis marks and brackets and setting off long quotations. Such a resource should be available in the writing center and tutors should be skilled in using it. The Purdue OWL is also an invaluable source on all aspects of writing honestly. Both Hacker and the Purdue OWL have helpful information on documentation styles for MLA and APA that is much more accessible than official manuals. The Purdue OWL handouts can be printed out and taken home by the writer for further work and assistance.

Complicating Matters

All of these points assume a situation in which writers have some sense of the early work to be done and know that they can come into the writing center for help with skills they're unsure of. Often, however, this is not the case. We've all seen frantic writers who come into the writing center with a paper that's due tomorrow. Help with introducing material from sources and documenting it properly is still possible of course. But what about the "patchwork quilt" papers that barely stitch together information lifted almost intact from sources? Options are limited, and it's possible none of them will be successful.

The writer needs to be asked about material that seems to be copied from sources. This can be done gently and politely—"Are these your words?"—but tutors need to communicate clearly that the consequences of plagiarism can be dire. Tutors should know the plagiarism policies of their own institutions so that they can be specific and not just hand out vague threats. I recommend that tutors urge the writer to check with the instructor or, if that's not possible, to get a second opinion from another tutor whenever there is a question about how the writer is using sources.

Students tend to have two responses to such advice. One is that the writer will simply leave—maybe not immediately but relatively soon. The writer hasn't received what she wants, so help will be sought elsewhere. Tutors should not consider this a failure on their part. The message has been given and received. Perhaps the writer will know better in the future. And if not, an essential lesson in tutoring as in life is that we have little control over the behavior of others.

A second, more positive possibility is that the writer will be eager or at least willing to work with the material for what it is: a work-in-progress. In truth this is what we often if not always see in the writing center, an early draft, ripe for revision. Writers don't always realize this initially, of course, and some aren't glad to hear it. But others will be. When this happens, the draft becomes a discovery draft with which to work, and the Twenty Questions (see Figure 17–1) can be very useful.

Set the draft aside so that the writer can break his strong connection to the language and structure of the source. Then work through the Twenty Questions, perhaps not all but those that seem useful. This will give the writer a chance to construct a framework on which to build an original paper. A similar approach is a variation of Peter Elbow's idea of the Instant Version.[9] The writer again sets aside all sources, notes, and drafts and simply writes a quick version of the paper, giving him a place to start. The results would have been better if these had been done earlier, of course, but this is an imperfect world and none of us always does what we should. We can still learn—and perhaps do better next time. The writing center maxim that we are not about better papers but better writers applies here.

Ultimately, it pays to remember that writing a good research paper takes practice. It's something like directing a chorus. Once the writer has found the sources, he must then give each of them a role or a voice in the chorus of different voices that will become his research paper. He can allow some to keep their own voices (direct quotes), but most of them must be blended with his own (paraphrases and summaries) to make the paper author-itative. When viewed in this way, we gain greater appreciation for what goes into a good research paper and a better understanding of how tutors can help.

Further Reading

Bowers, Neal. 1997. *Words for the Taking: The Hunt for a Plagiarist.* New York: Norton.

A fascinating account of a poet's search for the person plagiarizing his work, it gives fine insight into the state of mind of the one who is being plagiarized.

Bouman, Kurt. 2004. "Raising Questions About Plagiarism." In *ESL Writers*, eds. Shanti Bruce and Ben Rafoth, 105–16. Portsmouth, NH: Boynton/Cook.

This reading helps tutors to understand how American academic rules for documenting sources compare to other cultures' and offers ideas for how to talk with ESL writers about problems of plagiarism.

Moody, Pam. 1993. "Tutors' Column: A Slight Case of Plagiarism." *Writing Lab Newsletter* 17 (5): 9–11.

A tutor writes about the sense of betrayal and failure she experiences when a student with whom she is working plagiarizes a paper.

"Plagiarism in the Classroom: Readers Explain How They Define It and How They Deal with It." 1994. *The Council Chronicle* 3 (5): 14–15.

This is one way tutors can see the diversity of instructors' views and approaches to plagiarism, and a reminder that not all teachers see the matter in the same way. After

Research writing can be described as follows:

Gathering information ↔ Analyzing and synthesizing ↔ Communicating/writing

Daily writing will help you with a research paper more than anything else: Every day, take ten or fifteen minutes to answer one of the questions.

1. What topic have you chosen for your research and why?
2. What do you know now about the topic?
3. What do you want to find out?
4. Are you aware of any controversies regarding this topic? If so, what are they, and what is your current stand on the issue?
5. Have you noticed any areas of disagreement among your sources?
6. Which of the viewpoints seems the most valid to you? Why?
7. Do you have any unanswered questions at this point?
8. Did anything surprise you as you gathered information?
9. What has been the most interesting aspect of the material you've gathered so far?
10. After reviewing your data or sources, what do you see as the latest problems in the field of your topic?
11. What do you think are the important facts of the matter?
12. Are there better ways of interpreting the reported information that previous authors have ignored?
13. How can you relate these previous studies into a general picture?
14. What new insight can you contribute?
15. Considering all of the previous questions, how would you sum up your current attitude toward your topic in a sentence or two?
16. If you decide to use the answer to Question 15 as a working thesis for your paper, what information will you have to give your readers to convince them that your stand is a valid one? What questions of theirs will you have to answer? (The answers to these questions will suggest major points for your outline.)
17. What one real question will your paper answer?
18. What is your current answer to this question?
19. What information do you have to support this?
20. What information do you still need to gather?

Not all of these questions will work for all topics, of course, so use them to deal with whatever information and topics have been chosen. Go back to these questions at different points in the process and see how their answers change as more information is gathered and the topic is reexamined.

Figure 17–1. Twenty Questions for Research Writing

reading this article, writing center tutors might consider how their own faculty differ on the question of plagiarism. (*The Council Chronicle* is a newsletter published by the NCTE in Urbana, Illinois.)

Notes

1. Libby Miles, *Avoiding Plagiarism* (Handout from Purdue University Writing Lab, 1997).
2. Lisa Ede, "The Concept of Authorship: An Historical Perspective" (ERIC Document No. ED266481).
3. Thomas Mallon, *Stolen Words: Forays into the Origins and Ravages of Plagiarism* (New York: Ticknor & Fields, 1989), 24.
4. Miles.
5. Irene L. Clark, "Collaboration and Ethics in Writing Center Pedagogy," *Writing Center Journal* 9 (1) (1988): 8.
6. Kristin Walker, "Consulting with ESL Students in an Engineering Writing Center: Issues and Strategies for Dealing with the Problem of Plagiarism," *Writing Lab Newsletter* 21 (6) (1997): 3.
7. Walker, 2.
8. The Purdue OWL may be found at http://owl.english.purdue.edu/.
9. Peter Elbow, *Writing with Power* (New York: Oxford University Press, 1981), 64–65.

Works Cited

Clark, I. L. 1988. "Collaboration and Ethics in Writing Center Pedagogy." *Writing Center Journal* 9 (1): 3–12.

Ede, L. 1985. "The Concept of Authorship: An Historical Perspective." Speech/Conference Paper. ERIC Document No.: ED266481.

Elbow, P. 1981. *Writing with Power.* New York: Oxford University Press.

Genius Papers. Accessed 21 March 2005. http://geniuspapers.com/.

Hacker, D. 1999. *A Writer's Reference.* 4th ed. Boston: Bedford/St. Martin's.

Mallon, T. 1989. *Stolen Words: Forays into the Origins and Ravages of Plagiarism.* New York: Ticknor & Fields.

Miles, L. 1997. *Avoiding Plagiarism.* Handout from Purdue University Writing Lab.

Peter Elbow on Writing. 1995. Videocassette. Media Education Foundation.

Plagiarism.org. 1999. iParadigms, Inc. Accessed 21 March 2005. http://plagiarism.org/.

Purdue Online Writing Lab. 1999. Purdue University Writing Lab. http://owl.english.purdue.edu.

Walker, K. 1997. "Consulting with ESL Students in an Engineering Writing Center: Issues and Strategies for Dealing with the Problem of Plagiarism." *Writing Lab Newsletter* 21 (6): 1–5.

Contributors

Corinne Agostinelli is a marketing coordinator with Pennsylvania Financial Group in State College, Pennsylvania. She worked part-time as a peer writing consultant for a hospitality communications class at Pennsylvania State University, where she graduated in 1998 with a B.A. in English (emphasis in creative writing). Corinne spent two years as a writing tutor at Penn State and presented at both national and mid-Atlantic writing center conferences.

Wendy Bishop taught rhetoric and composition and creative writing at Florida State University (FSU), where she was Kellogg W. Hunt Distinguished Professor of English. She directed the writing center at the University of Alaska Fairbanks before moving to Tallahassee in 1989. From 1989 to 1992, she directed the first-year writing program at FSU. Wendy Bishop died November 21, 2003.

Carol Briam is a business communications specialist living in France. She has had a varied career as a newspaper reporter in Arizona, a teacher of English as a Foreign Language in West Africa, and a U.S. Foreign Service Officer in Asia. She has advanced degrees in management and economics, and is completing a Ph.D. in English composition and TESOL at Indiana University of Pennsylvania.

Kara Bui worked as an English peer tutor at the University of Michigan's Sweetland Writing Center for two years and received her B.S. degree in cellular molecular biology. During that time, she also managed communications between tutors and clients for Sweetland's Online Writing Laboratory.

George Cooper is a lecturer in the Sweetland Writing Center at the University of Michigan, where he teaches composition and peer tutoring, maintains an educational collaboration with a Detroit public high school, and pursues his interest in the history of composition.

Mary Mortimore Dossin taught writing at Plattsburgh State University of New York and trained and supervised the writing tutors there for many years. Mary Dossin hosted the National Conference on Peer Tutoring in Writing in 1998.

Carol Ellis is director of the writing center and writing programs at Claremont Graduate University. She earned her Ph.D. in English from the University of Iowa. Her interests include women's journal writing and creative nonfiction.

Alexis Greiner graduated from Rollins College, where she was an interdisciplinary studies major in biology, philosophy, and writing, and was a two-year veteran of the writing center. She was selected a Clough Consultant, a leader and example within the center, and was voted Writing Consultant of the Year in 1999. Alexis gave the keynote address at the National Conference on Peer Tutoring in Writing in Lexington, Kentucky, in 1997.

Muriel Harris has retired from her position as professor of English and the writing lab director at Purdue University, where she tutored and trained tutors for almost thirty years. She founded and continues to serve as editor of *The Writing Lab Newsletter*. Her brief grammar handbook, *Prentice Hall Reference Guide* (now in its sixth edition), and also *The Writer's FAQs* (Prentice Hall, second edition), a brief pocket manual, are both products of her writing center experience. Her articles, chapters, and conference presentations all reflect her commitment to the tutorial approach as the most effective way to help writers.

William J. Macauley Jr. directs the writing center and is an assistant professor of English at Mount Union College, where he also teaches courses in composition studies, community literacy/service-learning, and writing. He is editor of *IWCA Update*, the newsletter of the International Writing Centers Association. He earned his Ph.D. in English in 1999 in rhetoric and linguistics at Indiana University of Pennsylvania; his dissertation examined studio-based learning, student empowerment, and composition. He learned a great deal about how to teach writing from a long line of generous writing tutors.

Nicole Kraemer Munday teaches composition at Salisbury University, and she is currently completing her dissertation titled, "Peer Response Practices in a Freshman Resident Hall: An Ethnographic Study." Prior to her career in teaching, she worked as a journalist, focusing primarily on political reporting and feature writing. Her interest in the benefits of peer conferencing began during her time as a tutor at the College of William and Mary's writing resource center.

Helena Poch graduated from Pennsylvania State University in 1999 with a B.S. in nursing and a minor in world literature. Helena worked for the Penn State writing center for three-and-a-half years and presented at two national conferences. She continues to write and enjoys helping others realize their writing potential.

Ben Rafoth directs the writing center at Indiana University of Pennsylvania. He teaches courses in research methods and composition theory and pedagogy. His other publications include journal articles and books on teaching writing, including *ESL Writers* (2004), coedited with Shanti Bruce.

Linda Riker is a 1998 graduate of the University of Michigan, where she received a B.S. in Biology.

Jennifer J. Ritter teaches at the University of Alaska in Anchorage. Her specialty is second language writing and applied linguistics. She gained her first writing center experience at Indiana University of Pennsylvania, where she designed and developed IUP's first online writing center.

Elizabeth Santoro graduated from Pennsylvania State University in 1999 with a B.A. in international politics and a B.A. in French. At Penn State, she was a tutor and co-coordinator of the writing center.

Carol Severino directs the writing center at the University of Iowa, where she has recently helped to construct and direct a Writing Fellows (peer tutoring/writing across the curriculum) program. She researches and teaches about how culture and language background influence writing and pedagogy. She serves on the editorial boards of the *Journal of Second Language Writing, College Composition and Communication,* and *Writing Center Journal.*

Alice L. Trupe directs the writing center and teaches in the English department at Bridgewater College of Virginia. Her other writing and research interests revolve around the impact of electronic environments on genre and pedagogy.

Molly Wingate directed the Colorado College writing center before her retirement; she now coordinates the college's minor in nonviolence, organizing symposia, speakers' visits, and other special events. She is involved in the Pikes Peak Justice and Peace Commission. She helped to create a nonprofit foundation to raise money for Manitou Springs School District 14 and serves as the vice president of the board of trustees.

Beth Rapp Young directs the writing center at the University of Central Florida in Orlando, where she also teaches courses in writing, grammar, and research methods. In the past, she has directed or tutored in writing centers at the University of Alabama in Huntsville, Rollins College, and the University of Southern California. She has served on the board of the Southeastern Writing Centers Association and the National Conference on Peer Tutoring in Writing.

Pavel Zemliansky is an assistant professor of writing and rhetoric at James Madison University, where he teaches courses in composition, rhetorical theory, and computers and writing. He has coedited two books on research writing pedagogy (both with Wendy Bishop) and a book on application of computers to the teaching of professional writing (with Kirk St. Amant). He lives in central Virginia with his wife and son.

Index

171